# The Easy Inspiring Guide

# MONEY:

## Fall Down?  Get Up!

### Bonnie St. John

St. John Deane, Inc.
163 Amsterdam Avenue
Suite 135
New York, New York 10023-5001

www.bonniestjohn.com
(212) 580-0149

Printed in the United States of America
ISBN 0-9707146-3-7

This book is dedicated to the vision:

People talking and laughing,

Mastering their money,

Feeling their divinity and strength,

and

Prospering with peace and joy!

# Acknowledgements

How can I possibly thank everyone who has contributed? I appreciate the nurses and doctors who made me whole, my ski coaches and teachers, my family who made me strong…it takes a village to create an author!

In the immediate sense, I thank the producers of the Ricki Lake Show who went searching for a Money Expert and picked me. (Thanks, Lily Walters, for suggesting me to them!) My experience on Wall Street, on the White House economic team, and with a masters degree in economics from Oxford gave me the credentials, but it was my desire to teach money in an inspiring and step-by-step way that filled the need. I deeply felt called to empower women and boost their self-esteem where it counts: their wallets. What a challenge!

Thanks also to my buddies from the National Association of Women Business Owners who rolled up their sleeves, joined the team and helped birth this book: Suzanne Pease on graphic art and Diane Valletta, my editor. You shared my vision, felt my excitement and met my deadlines!

My friends across the country also shared my excitement and listened to my wacky ideas. You all brought me books to read, quotes to quote, and ideas to include: Dina, Howard, Sally, Darlyne, Bamie, Mom, David, and my daughter Darcy. Angela, thanks for supporting me through it. Grant, thanks for your true love and support-until death do us part.

Also to my beta-testers who read the book and commented on it and to those who gave time for interviews – I thank you deeply, though I cannot list all your names here. You all breathed life into the pages.

My family at Sponsors for Educational Opportunity in NYC also deserves some blame for this adventure: when you asked me to chair the SIRV Financial Literacy for Families Committee I had no idea it would take over my life! Your vision, integrity, values and support in this project were key. You all enrich my life. Michael and Maria – love you both.

To Olivia Mellan, Barbara Stanny, and Debtors Anonymous – thank you for sharing your quizzes. They have already provided a wake up call for many people.

Although I feel everyone mentioned here is part of my life's Abundance Party, I especially appreciate the ladies who did it with me by the book – Darlyne and Dina. Prospering with you for 60 Days was a highlight in my life!

I appreciate every day the love, support and wisdom of my business team: Washington Speakers Bureau – Bernie, Harry, Christine, Malinda and all the staff who allow me to travel the world inspiring people through speeches; and Sally at Zip Celebrity who sees the best in me; I thank you all. My financial advisors who keep the corporate finances or my personal finances on track: Michael, Ken, Linda, Jim, Dee, Marlene, Chris and Dick. Your encouragement helps me grow.

The love, support and guidance of my spiritual team lifts me up and gives me any true greatness I might contribute in the world: Susan Taylor, Debbi Fields, Montel Williams, Nido Quebein, Les Brown, and Tony Robbins, my spiritual mentors; Pastor Chuck and Marge from my church in Pine Valley, California; Pastor Justin of Unity NYC; Enid Singer, an angel; my mother, Ruby; my sister, April; my brother, Wayne; my daughter, Darcy; Grant and my New Zealand family; and all the ancestors on whose shoulders we stand. Thank You.

How can I possibly thank everyone who has contributed? My life has been touched by the thousands upon thousands of people I have met at events across the country, through television and radio, and through books. You inspire me.

# Contents

# Your Invitation to the Party

**ABUNDANCE:** *I'm so glad you're here! I've been trying to get your attention for ages!!*

**ME:** *Thanks. But WHO are YOU?*

**ABUNDANCE:** *Abundance. Divine Abundance. (Get it? Like "Bond. James Bond." I'm so cool!)*

**ME:** *Excuse me... have we met?*

**ABUNDANCE:** *I can't believe this. I'm with you everywhere. Every day of your life. And you don't even know me?! This is worse than I thought. We better get started right away.*

**ME:** *Started on what?*

**ABUNDANCE:** *The Easy, Inspiring Guide to Money.*

**ME:** *What's that?*

**ABUNDANCE:** *You give me 60 days. I show you how to make space for me, for Abundance, in your life. And YOU start down the road of infinite Prosperity, Peace, and Joy.*

*Basically, your life starts to change so you*
*MAKE MORE MONEY and HAVE MORE CASH IN THE BANK.*

*More peace. More joy. And a Healthy Self-Esteem.*

**ME:** *Is this going to be hard?*

ABUNDANCE: *Isn't what you're doing right now hard? Sheez! Anything has got to be easier. Actually, our journey is the easiest, most energizing and fun way there is to learn about money.*

ME: *Money? Fun?*

ABUNDANCE: *That's just the attitude that makes you hard to help. Money **should** be fun! ....and a source of joy and security.*

*Giving is fun. Shopping is fun. Hanging out with friends is fun. And then there are vacations, redecorating, collecting things, books, gardening - you name it.*

*So you see -Money is fun. But somewhere along the line you got the message that managing money was not fun. And you believed it.*

ME: *I always watched my parents struggling with the bills....*

ABUNDANCE: *I know, I know. In fact, I know everything. Trust me. This journey is going to be fun beyond your wildest imagination. But - there is one thing that could make it even better.*

ME: *What's that?*

ABUNDANCE: *Do it with someone else. Ask a friend or several friends to do it with you. If you're married, do it with your spouse. If you have kids, do some of the exercises as a family.*

*The more you share it with others ... the more you surround yourself with abundant feelings, thoughts and actions ... It's easier to stick with when you go through it together.*

ME: *But ... if I get some friends together, will I have to tell them embarrassing things about my money?*

**ABUNDANCE:** *Ever notice how much shame and fear you have about money? That's a prosperity killer right there. But actually, the answer is no. You only share what you want to share. You each get your own book and follow the daily exercises. You have five exercises each week and little bits of reading.*

*Then, once a week you get together and talk about what you did and learned that week. It's just hanging out time. You can meet at a coffee shop, walk around the lake, have a potluck with all the kids ... whatever.*

*Make it fun and appealing with people you want to spend time with. Call it a weekly "Abundance Party." You'll learn so much from the others. You'll reinforce what you learned by sharing it. AND - you'll get even more excited during the week knowing you can share the excitement.*

**ME:** *Excitement??? About saving and budgeting?*

**ABUNDANCE:** *You'll get excited about Freedom, Wealth and being the Master Of Your Own Universe! You'll see - sometimes you will get so excited, you can't wait for your Abundance Party to share. You just have to call and tell someone. If you have to travel and miss an Abundance Party, you'll even call in and attend by speaker phone.*

**ME:** *Is there a structure for the abundance party?*

**ABUNDANCE:** *You can start by giving each person six minutes to talk about their week of daily exercises. (time it)*

*They should talk about three things:*
*1. Say what they loved most.*
*2. Say what they want to focus on next week.*
*3. Ask for encouragement and feedback. Let the others help them remove any obstacles to staying on the journey.*

*Help them remove any obstacles to staying on the journey. Then, let the next person have a turn until everybody has a chance. At six minutes per person, you can cover up to four or five people in about half an hour. Then you have another half hour for an activity (these are listed in the book as you go).*

*As time goes by, you can reshape the structure of your abundance party to suit yourself. Add your own affirmations at the beginning and the end. If you don't like the suggested activity, pick an exercise from the book and do it together. Create your own ritual - like practicing giving to one another in little ways.*

ME:     *Wow. That sounds fun. And energizing!*

ABUNDANCE:   *Oh yeah. That's how miracles are made.*

ME:     *Ok, I'm gonna do it. It's only eight weeks. 60 days. Sounds like it would change my attitude toward money and bring abundance into my life. Ha! God knows I could use more money and less stress.*

ABUNDANCE:   *Before you start, take a minute and write down what you want to get out of this. After 60 days of focusing on your prosperity, what do you expect to be changed in your life?*

ME:     *Hmm. You mean my feelings? My thoughts? Or my actions?*

ABUNDANCE:   *Yeah. Any of those. What is dealing with money like for you now and how do you expect it to be different?*

Use this space here to write down the changes you want to happen in your life:

*Pay all my bills, reduce my debt, increase my savings and support my kids with their education expenses*

Read over your thoughts. Write one sentence in the space below that paints a picture of you at the end of the journey:

*debt free*

Achieving these changes or better is your "Mission" for the next 60 days. **Okay? Fasten your seat belt and let's do it!!!!!!**

# OVERVIEW OF THIS BOOK

---

"There's only one thing
you need to know about accounting
...and they don't teach you this
at Harvard Business School:

Cash in
Must exceed
Cash out."

—Terry Allen, author of *No Cash, No Fear*, is a graduate of
the Harvard Business School and was called a "chronic
entrepreneur" in a case study on his many successes.

---

This is a very simple book.
We will cover only three things:
**Money In, Money Out and Money Supports Me.**
That's the whole deal.

Make sure more money comes in than goes out.
It's pretty simple.

We could use fancy words like income, spending, and saving,
but it's really just about

**Money In,  Money Out  and Money Supports Me.**

# HOW TO USE THIS BOOK

1. **Trust the Process.** The exercises build on each other and begin creating miracles in your wallet!

2. **DAILY: Each day has an exercise or quiz to do.** Sure, you can work ahead if you have time, or catch up if you get behind. Some days are super easy. Others may require a bit more thought. Just take it one day at a time.

3. **WEEKLY: Each week starts with a short article to read.** This will get you thinking about the topic we'll be working on during the week.

   **Day 6 is for your action plan.** You get a chance to look over the actions you have decided to take-the Page of Promises to Myself (last page of the book)-and put them on your calendar or to do list. Action makes change happen.

   **Day 7 is for your Abundance Party.** Of course, you can do the party on whatever day works with your schedule. If you are doing the book on your own, still treat yourself to an Abundance Party by setting aside time to reflect on your progress and doing the activity. If you want someone to join you partway through, it's okay even if you are at different parts of the book. Meeting regularly with a friend or two makes the journey more fun – and more prosperous!

4. **SECTIONS: There are three sections-Money In, Money Out, and Money Supports Me.** Over weeks 1 to 3, we'll be covering Money In. We'll cover Money Out in weeks 4, 5, and 6. Money Supports Me is in weeks 7 and 8.

5. **CONCLUSION: Days 57 to 60 are for celebrating your progress, enjoying new prosperity and envisioning your future!** Don't forget to get in touch and let me know the wonderful things that happen in your life on this journey together. Contact me at bonnie@bonniestjohn.com or (212) 580-0149. There will be prizes for great stories that we want to share!

### Ready or not....Here we go!

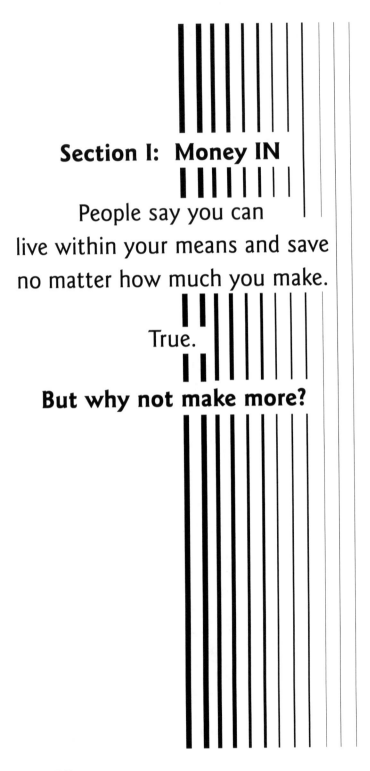

## Section I: Money IN

People say you can

live within your means and save

no matter how much you make.

True.

**But why not make more?**

# Theme:
# Jumpstart Your Prosperity Engine
# With Self-Hypnosis

People wonder…
"How the heck
does a **one-legged, black girl** from San Diego
end up going to the Olympics
and **winning medals in ski racing?**"

It seems **impossible**.
Being disabled from birth,
I had **no image** of myself as an athlete.
I was even exempt from PE in high school.
There were **no** African-American,
Olympic-ski-medallist **role models**.
I was the first.
In San Diego, there was **no snow**.

It seems impossible…

# Inner Wealth Hypnosis:
# The Secret of My Success

How do you do things that seem impossible to most people?
The secret of my success is Self-Hypnosis.
It's easy to do.
I will teach you my own method: **Inner Wealth Hypnosis.**

I used Inner Wealth Hypnosis as a sales rep for IBM.
I overcame my fears of rejection and won awards for innovation.

I used Inner Wealth Hypnosis as an inspirational speaker.
It's what 75% of people say they fear more than death.
I am one of the top women speakers in the nation,
paid fabulous fees for telling my stories and inspiring people.
Named one of the five most inspiring women in America
by NBC Nightly News.

I used Inner Wealth Hypnosis while working on Wall Street
and in the White House to keep up with the best of the best!
I used the same technique to help in childbirth!

This one simple technique for self-hypnosis
will allow you to create the  inner wealth and inner strength
you need to do impossible things.

If I can overcome the limitations I thought I had:
Losing a leg. Having no snow. Having no money.
And being the only black person in ski racing at my level.

If I can do that
you can use this technique to overcome
whatever baggage you have
about creating wealth in your life
and creating peace and security around money.

I am so excited to share this with you!!!!

Money goes up and down - but inner wealth is always there.
You become wealthy when you strengthen your inner feelings.
And they don't swing up and down
depending on how much money you have in the bank.

"Let us learn to think of dollars, as we do of leaves on trees, or oranges, as the natural and inevitable result of the active law within," says Joel Goldsmith, author of *The Infinite Way*. There is truly no need to be concerned even when trees appear to be bare, he explains, as long as we know that the tree is being fertilized, watered and exposed to sunshine. In the same way, our finances may be high or low. But if we are continuing to water them with attention, clarity and willingness to seize opportunities, they will bear fruit. Leaves come and go with the seasons, but the tree always has abundance.

Similarly, money will come and go.
We will have ups and downs in the economy.
You will have problems.
You will face challenges — but when you have inner wealth and inner strength, you are always able to get up when you fall down and create more wealth again.

**So, here it is—ENJOY!!**

# Inner Wealth Hypnosis
# Directions

Before you begin —

Write down any reasons why you do not have the life of prosperity, joy and purpose you would like to have now:

*Children's father lost job & hasn't been able to support them for a year. I had all savings & credit to keep them/us afloat. My salary isn't enough to cover it all.*

What you wrote above are beliefs in your limits. Pick one and turn it on its head. Below, write down the complete and total opposite of it. Make it positive and unlimited.

> • For example, if you wrote, "I don't have enough money," reverse it to "I have more than enough money — more than I can use or spend!"

> • If you wrote: "My skills don't pay much," write the unlimited version as "I know enough to be a millionaire," or "My skills make me wealthy."

> • If you wrote: "I don't want to work harder for more money," write the no limits version as "I play, have fun expressing myself, and create mega wealth!"

**Write your UNLIMITED belief here:**

*I make more than enough money to support my family - so much so that I am able to save!*

12     Money IN!

# Inner Wealth Hypnosis
## Step-by-step

Here's exactly how to do it—

Once you've rewritten your limiting belief into an unlimited belief, find a comfortable spot where you can close your eyes and think and day-dream. (Sometimes the only place is the bathroom. Your car can be good too – when parked!) Have pen and paper ready. Read the following instructions all the way through and then try it.

**STAIRS:** Imagine you're walking down a long staircase with 30 stairs. Count down from 30 as you walk down. When you get to the bottom, imagine two doors.

**RIGHT DOOR:** Go through the door on your right and enter a place that feels really great. It could be a tropical beach, a family reunion, a romantic dinner – your special feel-good zone. Enjoy the sites, sounds and textures of this place. What are you wearing? What can you smell?

**LEFT DOOR:** Once you are relaxed and feeling good, see yourself going back out the first door and entering into the second door. Here you will see your inner self. You can imagine a mirror or being with a separate person who is your inner self. Your inner self may look different than you do.

**GIVE LOVE TO YOUR INNER SELF:** Now greet yourself with love and joy. You know how a dog acts when its master comes home. Treat yourself like that. Give yourself a hug. Give yourself flowers or jewelry. Something different every time you come down to visit.

**SAY YOUR UNLIMITED BELIEF:** Next, tell your inner self the unlimited belief you wrote down. Open your eyes and read it if you need to. Then imagine your inner self saying the same unlimited belief back to you.

**RECEIVE LOVE**: Now imagine you're getting love from your inner self. If you believe in God, a higher power or universal wisdom, imagine love coming from there. Open yourself to this experience of love and feel whatever comes up.

**SAY YOUR UNLIMITED BELIEF:** Repeat your unlimited belief again.

**ASK:** Ask your inner self (or God, higher power, universal love, collective consciousness, etc.) for wisdom. "What do I need to know today?"

**LISTEN:** Write down whatever comes in to your mind. Sometimes I have so much static and chaos in my head, I have to say to myself "I am listening" several times before my mind calms down. Write what you hear.

**SAY THANKS:** Hug yourself. Express your appreciation and say goodbye. Open your eyes, refreshed and ready for more prosperity coming your way.

**READ YOUR NOTES:** This last step is very important. Scan over your notes, pick out what you think is valuable and toss out what is not. Not everything that pops in to your head is divine inspiration! Some things are just junk. Is it loving? Is it wise?

**What To Do With What You Get:** It's a good idea to use a trusted friend as a sounding board to help you decide what is junk and what's not. I don't advise taking big risks or doing anything crazy just because it pops into your head. Often the best ideas are very simple. I often hear advice like "get some sleep," or "do your paperwork." I get so excited about the big projects that I need reminding to do the little things.

Some of the most important action items will come up later. You may suddenly think, "I should call so-and-so." Or, "I should go to that place." Or, "I should help this person."

Obey these requests from your intuition – as quickly as you can! Often, they lead to a new and better job, a business opportunity or prosperity in other forms. They can be a quick shortcut you might never have logically figured out.

When you tune in to your intuition, calm your mind, and plant prosperity beliefs, your mind will work to give you these connections that you could not have come up with any other way. Listen as the day goes on … and honor the ideas that come up.

*[Note: We will be practising this extensively this week. It will get you going in the right direction. In this abundance journey, it is JUST ONE of the tools in our kit that we will use from time to time…you aren't required to do it every day. You can, however, do it as much or as little as you like. Do it anywhere-like waiting for appointments or before getting out of your car.]*

6/2:
Answer: It will be okay.

# Inner Wealth Hypnosis

Limited Belief: *I don't make enough money to support my family.*

Unlimited Belief:
*I make more than enough money to support my family, so much so that I am able to save.*

What I saw:

On the stairs—

Inside the right door—

*Islamorada*

Inside the left door—

*Bruised Souls*

Listening:

What I need to know today—

*everything will be okay. This is temporary*

Circle the good stuff – put action items on your
Page of Promises to Myself (last page)

# Inner Wealth Hypnosis

Limited Belief:

Unlimited Belief:

What I saw:

    On the stairs—

    Inside the right door—

    Inside the left door—

Listening:

    What I need to know today—

Circle the good stuff – put action items on your
Page of Promises to Myself (last page)

# Inner Wealth Hypnosis

Limited Belief:

Unlimited Belief:

What I saw:

    On the stairs—

    Inside the right door—

    Inside the left door—

Listening:

    What I need to know today—

Circle the good stuff – put action items on your
Page of Promises to Myself (last page)

# Inner Wealth Hypnosis: Why It Works

The Inner Wealth hypnosis technique
contains five different elements.

## 1. Visualization

Studies show visualizing relaxes the brain and helps you move into a subconscious state. Being in that state and bypassing some of your conscious mind allows you to plant ideas more firmly and reprogram the deeper subconscious. That's why we imagine walking down the stairs. It distracts your conscious mind and activates your subconscious.

## 2. Emotionalization

Going into the right door and having a feel-good experience activates your positive emotional state. Positive thinking doesn't work well without positive feeling. You can think yourself silly and you won't really change. It's the good feelings and emotions that really create change. In our usual busy state, we're not connected with our feelings at all. Shifting gears from that state into this feel-good place again creates the conditions we need to reprogram our subconscious.

## 3. Self-esteem

Inside the left door, giving and receiving love with your inner self boosts self-esteem. That's crucial for building wealth. People go into debt when they don't think a lot of themselves. When they don't take care of themselves. People who really love themselves do not go into debt – and they manage their money. Contributing to your self-esteem is another very important element of building wealth.

## 4. Drawing on the divine in you.

Connecting with the wisdom that comes from your inner self (or whatever divine forces you believe in) allows you to go beyond what your conscious mind knows and what it can do for you. It allows you to jump over some of the struggle and difficulty we have when we rely simply on what we know and our past experiences. It also allows you to have a little more peace when you don't feel it's all on your shoulders. A conscious struggle is not always required – because sometimes the answers don't come that way! We need to balance between working hard and surrendering to the divine.

## 5. Activating intuition

When you add up all these pieces – visualization, good feeling, self-esteem and drawing on the divine – you activate intuition. You plant the unlimited belief and then let the intuition continue to operate long after you finish the meditation. During the day ideas, connections, and opportunities will jump out at you. Some of them you will understand immediately as a new opportunity. Other ideas will seem completely disconnected until you follow through and realize "Aha!"

## 6. Shifting Focus

After planting the idea deep in your subconscious, you'll notice things differently. This is just common sense - not some kind of metaphysical thing. When your mind is more focused on your opportunities and your beliefs in the unlimited, you start to see confirmation of that in the world.

Whatever we believe at the subconscious level, we confirm for ourselves in the world. If you think people hate you, you are going to see evidence of that in the world. If you believe people love you, you are going to see evidence of that in the world. We tend to focus on what we believe in. By planting the unlimited belief, you start to notice evidence of that belief in the world.

**Question:** If this is really so powerful, why isn't everyone doing it?

**Answer:** Wealth makers ARE doing it. People who create wealth have their own rituals, routines, or habits that bring their inner wealth into gear – even when the outer world shows no evidence of prosperity. Not all wealth creators go through steps like this inner wealth hypnosis technique. But rest assured that they know how to connect with a deep source inside themselves, one that unleashes their power to create wealth. You may be one of these people. Learning to consciously activate your inner wealth could reduce the stress you feel in the ups and downs with money.

Wealth creators have a deep belief in their own value, unlimitedness, and prosperity. Some may have these positive habits because of the way they were brought up. They may not have to do many steps because they don't have to overcome the negative programming that I (and you, too?) received in childhood. It may look easier for other people, but they are taking water from the same well.

People who are tied to a scarcity mindset will not do this. If they ever read The Inner Wealth Hypnosis Technique, they might try it once, and then forget about it. They are continuously seeing opportunities for wealth and prosperity and refusing to believe them. Pretending they aren't there. Avoiding them. Using their own beliefs and limits to screen out these opportunities.

Imagine telling a scientist in 1890 that a beam of light could cut through metal or play music. Or do surgery on the eye... He would laugh at you because he cannot understand a laser beam.

You, however, are reading this because you want to have prosperity and peace in your life. You know there is greatness in you. Given the key to your inner wealth, you will use it – and learn to use it effectively. You are one of the few people who can fathom the riches available to you through The Inner Wealth Hypnosis. Practice it wisely and make it your own.

# Get Your
# ABUNDANCE PARTIES
# Going!!

## What would be fun?

How many people? Do you want to do it by yourself? One to one with a friend or spouse? In a group of friends? I wouldn't recommend more than 6 or 7 people – more than that and each person doesn't get enough time. What would be fun for you?

## Where would be fun?

At home? A coffee shop? At work on a lunch break? Walking and talking? By phone conference? (two people with 3-way calling can get four people on the phone!)

## Who would be fun?

Fun is crucial. I didn't ask who you think you SHOULD do it with or COULD do it with. Who is fun? Who would you look forward to seeing? Who really wants more prosperity?

## When can you invite these people to participate?

Put it on your schedule.

## When can you start getting together?

Put it on your schedule. Don't worry if you get ahead or behind in the book. You don't have to be synchronized.

## When will you do your daily exercises and reading?

Put it on your schedule.

This exercise may seem to be purely practical. But there's more. You're envisioning having fun and talking about money and prosperity. You're figuring out what fun and money means to you...so prosperity is already starting to unfold!

You're thinking about the people in your life who are willing to show up and drink coffee together in order to have more prosperity. You start realizing that some people say they want abundance, but aren't even willing to hang out with you and talk about it. This by itself is very educational.

Some people would do it, but you know they always make you feel dumb, discouraged or tired. You have a choice! Invite people who bring out only the best in you.

As you start to explain to other people what they will get and why you want to do it...it starts to happen!

You are affirming prosperity – preparing a place and time for abundance to find you. You are letting others know what you want. Heck, some people may say "No, thanks" to the parties but let you know about a great opportunity. Who knows?

By talking about the Abundance Parties with friends, you are committing to yourself and your prosperity. Once you start talking about it, it's harder to back down or give up on it. From the moment you make your commitment to prosperity, it starts to happen.

## Exercise: *Energize Your Abundance Party*

Briefly do the Inner Wealth Hypnosis. Don't worry about taking an unlimited belief with you. But, when you go into the feel-good place, see yourself at an Abundance Party...imagine good energy, good friends, and yourself sharing the news about your increasing prosperity attitude – and how that changes your life! Then, go visit your inner self. Just to stay in touch. Ask for wisdom. Listen.

# GIVE THANKS
# For What You Have

## Exercise: *Feeling Rich*

If you are reading this, you are probably in the top 1% of the wealthiest people on the planet. Think about that!

Gratitude and appreciation are like water on a plant.
The more gratitude you pour on, the bigger the plant grows.
Pour some gratitude and appreciation
on the wonderful gifts you have in your life now.
Watch them grow into more and more abundance.

**List ten things that make you feel rich in your life now:**
(You can include health, friendships, and non-monetary blessings as well as material things…like indoor plumbing!)

Practice feeling wealthy with the things you have now.
Walk yourself through the Inner Wealth Hypnosis.
Carry this message to your inner self:
**"I am already wealthy!"**

## Exercise: *Review Your Page of Promises to Myself*
(last page)

• Anything that has expired or is done…cross it out!

• Rewrite promises if you still want to do them and haven't done them yet.

• Look at anything you haven't done and put it on your calendar or To-Do list…figure out when you have time to get it done.

• Things you have successfully completed, cross out in a pretty color or put stars across them.

• Feel the feeling of what it means to you to have accomplished this promise to yourself and what a difference it makes in your life.

• Imagine how your life would be in the future if you hadn't done it. And then imagine how your life is different because you have done it.

• Think of a way to celebrate… Maybe calling a friend and sharing your accomplishment…. Or writing a thank you note to yourself!

# FIRST ABUNDANCE PARTY!!

(You can move this to any other day this week.)

*Yea! You made it through the first week!*
Can you feel the changes starting already? More Energy, Excitement, and Optimism about money?

Start the party with a quote, blessing or a song.

Choose a person to be the timekeeper.

Give each person six minutes to share
their week of daily Money IN exercises:

1. Say what they loved most.
2. Say what they want to focus on next week.
3. Ask for encouragement and feedback. Let the others help them remove any obstacles to staying on the journey.

Then, let the next person have a turn until everybody has a chance to share.

## Activity: *Letting go of old beliefs*

Have each person write an old, limiting belief about money on a piece of paper.

*Take Turns:*
Read your limiting money belief.
Tear it up, burn it or cut it with scissors.

Have everyone write the reverse – an unlimited belief about money – on a piece of paper you can put in your wallet.

*Take Turns:*
Read your new, unlimited belief.
Put it in your wallet.

(Carry it around with your money.
Read it from time to time
as you spend money.)

You're done!
Enjoy your friends.
***Savor your Abundance!***

# Theme:
# **Remembering the Past**
# **and**
# **Redesigning the Future**

I went to the **Paralympics** to compete as a **ski racer** in 1984.
It was in Innsbruck, Austria.

There were athletes
from 33 different countries – over 500 of them,
all there to see who was the **best of the best**.

I was racing on one ski against other women with one leg.
I had trained for **many, many, many years**
leading up to this one week of competition.

I was just so happy to be representing my country and have my team
jacket – it was the **fulfillment of a dream**…

# Bonnie's Story:  Fall Down? Get Up!

My mother came to watch me race. Actually, it was the first time my mother had seen me compete as a ski racer. We didn't have a lot of money when I was growing up. So she hadn't been able to fly from San Diego to Montana and Colorado and other places to see me race. At the Paralympics was the first time my mother was going to see me in a ski race.

Now, you have to understand here – my mother is the kind of person who doesn't really get it about sports. She is a school teacher, you know? If she sees a jogger on the street, she'll say, "Can't they do something constructive with that energy?" She just doesn't get it.

But she came to the Paralympics. And it happened. When I finished the first run of the slalom race, my time was the fastest in the world! I was in first place after the first run. My mother started jumping up and down and screaming:  "I get it – it's about WINNING!!!!"  My brother actually knocked her over and rolled her in the snow to cool her off.

But before I could really win, I had to go and do it again. It takes two runs, combined time to win a medal. I needed to get away from my mother because she was making me nervous, with all her hysterics. (You know how Moms can be.) So I went back up to the top of the race course to focus.

As I'm waiting my turn, I hear a rumor that there was a bad patch of ice on the course – a really horrible rut – and the first couple of women on the course had already fallen and crashed at this one spot. So I'm thinking … No heroics. I just need to have a good solid run and I can win.

I get in the starting gate. My stomach's doing back flips. And the race official starts counting down… 5 … 4 … 3 … 2 … 1
I push off out of the starting gate.
I'm hitting the red and the blue poles,
going down,
just focused on each turn,
and I get to where I can see the finish line…
I think to myself, "I've made it, I'm over the ice! I'm going to win!"

**That's when I hit the ice.**
I tried to dig in and hold on to my edge, but I couldn't do it.
WHAM! – I was on my rear end in the snow.
Man, I was so disappointed!
Have you ever screwed up when everybody in the world is watching?
It was painful.
But before I even realized what I was doing,
I was through the gate and over the finish line.
My reflexes took over.
**My reflexes, my training,**
**told me to get up and finish the race.**

When the dust cleared, I was in third place!
**I won the Bronze Medal!**
I got to stand on the winner's podium
with the US flag waving behind me.
I got to have the medal put around my neck by Swedish royalty …
my mother sobbing in the snow!

But none of it would have happened
if I hadn't gotten up and finished the race.
I thought about the woman who won
– she had also fallen and gotten up.
I realized she didn't beat me by skiing faster than me
– I had beaten her time in the first run.
I was probably skiing faster than her in the second run,
until I fell.
**She beat me – NOT by skiing faster,**
**but by GETTING UP FASTER.**

Everybody in life falls down.
To win, you have to get up.
To win the gold, sometimes you just have to get up a little faster.

## It's the same way with money.

There's a man I admire very much because
he fell down financially and picked himself up again.
His fall started in a simple way.
He borrowed money to lend to a friend who needed it.
His friend never paid him back.
When he couldn't pay back the loan himself,
he ended up in a bankruptcy.
He was selling real estate at the time,
and the real estate market started to fall away.
He ended up with no house and divorced from his wife.
He ended up sleeping on the sofa of a friend
and paying rent to do it.

One of the most painful experiences he described was
two years in a row when his daughter's birthday came around
and he couldn't afford to buy her any present at all.
The shame he felt was worse than any of his personal problems.

That pain, in part, fueled him to do the work he needed to do
and get his life back together.
After several jobs didn't work out
and he started a business that failed,
he went back into real estate sales
and committed himself to doing whatever it took
to earn money and get back on his feet.
Because of his failed business, he had over $50,000 of debt
And couldn't declare bankruptcy a second time.
"Real estate," he said,
"Was what I knew I could do and make money."
He worked longer hours than ever before in his life.
He drove a horrible beat-up car that he had to park around the corner
when showing houses to hide it from his clients.
Windows were missing.
The driver's side door didn't open.
He pushed himself to sell real estate, pay off his debts,
get some savings, and get back on his feet.

He was so proud when he was able to say to his daughter,
"For your birthday, I'm taking you to Hawaii for a week!"
He booked the tickets, booked the hotel,
and knew where the money was coming from.
I don't how much it meant to his daughter,
but I know for him,
the trip made up for a lot of shame
and humiliation he had suffered.
I asked him,
"What does it take to get up after you've fallen down that far?"
He said one of the most powerful things I have ever heard,

"Looking back I see that bad things would happen to me
– like a bad loan, a bad real estate market or a failed job –
and I let it affect my self worth.
I would get depressed and be unable to look for a new job
or find a way to make more money."
Getting knocked down wasn't the biggest problem—
It was getting depressed about it
that stopped him from getting up
and responding quickly in a positive way.

"I still have those feelings.
When something goes wrong I feel really really bad.
So I put this saying on my wall to remind myself what's going on:

**SHAME**-**Sh**\*t **H**appens **A**ffecting **M**y **E**steem."

It's a reminder that stuff happens to everybody
– everybody falls down.
It doesn't mean there's anything wrong with you.

The trick is getting up. And the faster you can get up,
the less the problems are going to grow in size.
Problems tend to snowball - the debt turns into bankruptcy,
and the bankruptcy turns into loss of housing, loss of car,
and that turns into loss of work and other problems.
So, the faster you can get up after something goes wrong financially,

the better off you are.
The key for my friend was understanding how
what happened to him in his money
affected his emotions and his esteem.
That was the real problem…
not what was happening with the money.
We all know money is emotional.
We bring a lot of baggage to it and a lot of history.
People would rather talk about their sex lives
than what goes on with their money.
It's more sensitive. More embarrassing. More upsetting.
But you have to be willing
to feel these funny, uncomfortable feelings
So you can move on.

When you refuse to face these feelings, you get stuck.
When you let them out, they fade away
And leave room for healthy, wealthy feelings.
Healthy, wealthy feelings are ABSOLUTELY necessary
Before you can start living a healthy, wealthy money life.

**So how do you do it?**

# Let's break it down!

# Week 2 ➡ Money IN ⬅ Day 1

## Exercise: *Past Memories*

What do you remember from your childhood about money coming in? Did money vary with the seasons? Was it always the same? Could your parents control how much money came in? Did your mother earn? Did your father earn? How did it change?

## Exercise: *NOW vs. THEN*

Is **money coming in** now like money came in when you were a kid? What is similar in your life now about how money comes in? What do you notice? Do you treat your employer like you treated your parents? Does your employer treat you like your parents did?

## Exercise:  *Limiting Beliefs*

Re-read the memories you wrote and what is similar about **money coming in** now. What are your limiting beliefs about **money coming in**? What do you accept that you don't want to?  Think about your behavior. What must be in your beliefs to make you do that?

## Exercise:  *Limit-BUSTING Beliefs*

Pick one of your limiting beliefs about money coming in and reverse it. Write out the opposite as if it were completely untrue, completely and totally untrue. For example, if you feel you have no control about how much money you get, write down:  "I generate money."  Say it out loud.

**Take your new, unlimited belief about money coming in and do your Inner Wealth Hypnosis.  Write your notes here:**

## Exercise: *Future Memories*

Read over the new beliefs you wrote down on yesterday's exercise. Close your eyes and imagine a time in the future. What is it like with your new belief? Imagine a specific time and place. What is happening to you? Imagine it in detail. Open your eyes and write down what you saw in your future memory.

Do your Inner Wealth Hypnosis using this future memory inside the right door – your feel-good place. Write your notes here about any ideas or wisdom that come up:

### *Anything you want to add to your Promises Page?*

## Exercise: *Review Your Page of Promises to Myself*
(last page)

• Anything that has expired or is done…cross it out!

• Rewrite promises if you still want to do them and haven't done them yet.

• Look at anything you haven't done and put it on your calendar or To-Do list…figure out when you have time to get it done.

• Things you have successfully completed, cross out in a pretty color or put stars across them.

• Feel the feeling of what it means to you to have accomplished this promise to yourself and what a difference it makes in your life.

• Imagine how your life would be in the future if you hadn't done it. And then imagine how your life is different because you have done it.

• Think of a way to celebrate….Maybe calling a friend and sharing your accomplishment…. Or writing a thank you note to yourself!

# SECOND ABUNDANCE PARTY!!

(You can move this to any other day this week.)

Yea! You made it through the 2nd week!
You are facing up to old feelings, getting in touch with your power to bring in money and reprogramming your brain!

Start the party with a quote, blessing or a song.

Choose a person to be the timekeeper.

Give each person six minutes to share
their week of daily Money IN exercises:

1. Say what they loved most.
2. Say what they want to focus on next week.
3. Ask for encouragement and feedback. Let the others help them remove any obstacles to staying on the journey.

Then, let the next person have a turn until everybody has a chance to share.

## SECOND ABUNDANCE PARTY!!

### Activity: *Getting in the flow*

Suze Orman, author of *The Courage to Be Rich*, says one of the most important ways to open ourselves to receive more money is to make sure we give on a regular, monthly basis. She tried an experiment with new financial clients who weren't doing so well. She asked some to start donating money to a place they felt good about giving to. Others she left alone. "I couldn't believe the results," writes Suze in *Suze Orman's Financial Guidebook*. "The better people felt about themselves from giving, and the more they kept their hands open to receive by relinquishing money, the more their financial situation improved."

Take a few minutes for everyone to think quietly about how much you have and how much you could give monthly (without causing self-deprivation). Think of a charity or faith-based organization you care deeply about. Commit to giving the money every month. Put a note in your bills or set up an automatic payment.

If you already give regularly, just focus your thoughts on the difference you are making and feel proud. It is easy to go on automatic pilot and forget to feel the joy of it. If you don't feel proud, consider changing where your donation goes.

Take turns sharing how your donation makes a difference in the world. It doesn't matter whether it is a lot or a little — you become part of a team when you give. Feel the feeling of being able to give money and make a difference.

You are a philanthropist!

# Theme:
# **MORE MONEY FOR YOU!**

ABUNDANCE: *Hi, it's Divine Abundance here.*

ME: *Hi, how are you?*

ABUNDANCE: *Abundant, like totally, and you?*

ME: *Well, I've got ups and downs - you know?*

ABUNDANCE: *I do know. I know everything. But here's the catch: I keep try-ing to give you what you want. But I get a lot of mixed signals from you.*

*Would you just tell me how much money you need every month to make it through the whole year with the peace and harmony that is your birthright?*

*Make it really clear how much you really need, and then we'll work on it together. Okay?*

**ME:**    *Wow! I'm all choked up.*

**ABUNDANCE:** *I'm always here for you - but you never ask. You keep pretending you don't really need much, but I see your pain. Don't minimize your needs. Remember insurance for your car and your loved ones ... retirement money ... dental, medical and vision too. You really can't have peace of mind in human form without all kinds of coverage.*

*I mean I can come through for you in a crisis, but it's so stressful that way. And then you always forget to ask for help when you get stressed - which makes it even harder for me to help. So please, tell me how much money you need. Be definite and clear, no waffling. And then ask me to help.*

*One more thing – this is important: be open and willing to try opportunities I bring to you. I can only work with you and through you.*

**ME:**    *I'm not always so good at being open and willing.*

**ABUNDANCE:** *You can ask for help with the being open and willing part too. Lots of humans need that.*

**ME:**    *Yeah, I sure do.*

**ABUNDANCE:** *Just ask. And don't forget, my love for you is infinite.*

# Exercise:    *My Letter To The Universe*

*Dear World,*
*To care and feed the temple of my soul and maintain the illusion of separateness*
*called my personality, I need money!*

## Each month I HAVE TO PAY:

(List your monthly ESSENTIAL expenses in the categories below. If you don't
know exact amounts, just guess.  Don't stress over this.)

For debt repayment:                                                              $ _____

For housing expenses
(rent/mortgage, utilities, cable, etc.)                                          $ _____

For living expenses (lunch money, clothes, dry cleaning,
groceries, transportation, retirement savings, etc.)                             $ _____

(Add up monthly necessities and write total here)    **Total #1** $_____

## Each month I WANT TO SPEND:

(List your OPTIONAL EXPENSES below. Think about eating out, entertain-
ment, extra clothes/shoes for fun, other special activities, church/charity, etc.
If you don't know exact amounts, just guess. Don't stress over this.)

(Add up monthly spending wants and write total here) **Total #2** $_____

(My Total Monthly Spending: Add  Totals #1 & #2) **Total #3** $ _____

**Each year I also HAVE TO PAY & WANT TO SPEND in extra ways:**
(List expenses that only happen once a year or less often than monthly.
Don't forget vacations, holiday gifts, birthdays, insurance, dental, etc. If you
don't know exact amounts, just guess. Don't stress over this. Just do it!)

(Add up yearly extras and write total here)   **Total #4** $_____

(Compute amount needed each month for
  yearly extras -divide Total# 4 by 12)   **Total #5** $_____

(Add Totals #3 and #5)   **Total #6** $_____

Add a cushion (lovably-human error), say 10 percent
  (Take 10% of Total #6 and write it here)   **Total #7** $_____

**Grand Total: Money I need every month after taxes**
               ( Total #6 plus Total #7)  $_____

*Thank you Abundant Universe for providing me with an after-tax income of*

$_____ *(fill in Grand Total) every month.*

**I feel loved and cared for!**

With gratitude,

_____
*(Sign your name here)*

If your Grand Total is less than your monthly pay after all the taxes are taken out – Congratulations!  You are saving, giving, paying your bills and doing everything you want on your current salary.

For most people, however, the opposite is true. They are not able to buy everything they need and still save, donate and pay for all the insurance they should have. It is easy to live **hoping** that someday you can afford to have all your needs met. Yet mostly people are not honest with themselves about what they really need.

Now that you have courageously looked at what you need – just to live in peace and security at your current standard of living – you are ready to start finding ways to get your needs met!

# Week 3 ➡ Money IN ⬅ Day 2

## Exercise: *Believing, feeling, focusing*

The process of bringing in the money starts by believing it is possible ... feeling how good it feels ... and focusing your attention on it. These internal, wealthy feelings act like a net to catch fish. Without a net, you stay hungry while fish swim all around you. With the right internal programming, you can easily scoop up all the opportunities for making money that you need. Don't believe me? Try it and see.

*(This process is very powerful - and it works. So you may want to go back and get more accurate numbers. Make sure you ask for enough!)*

- Close your eyes and clearly ask out loud for the universe, God or whatever you believe in to help you receive $_____ every month.

- Say out loud "*I, (your name), am willing and open to receive at least* $_____ *every month.*" Imagine how you feel when this amount is available to you every month.

- Write on a piece of paper or Post-it: "*(Your name) receives at least* $_____ *every month!*"

- Put it where you will see it every day and remember to feel it — not just think it.

- Do your Inner Wealth Hypnosis. Carry the message to your inner self: *I receive at least* $_____ *every month.*

## Exercise: *Ways To Increase Income*

List ten ideas for bringing in the money you need each month!

*This page is your brainstorm session with Abundance about how to raise your income to meet your needs. Remember: Abundance is everywhere. Your best friend, your banker, even people you don't like, all contain the divine abundance of the universe. Put down every idea that comes to you from anywhere – without judging it. Pick people's brains. Ask for ideas. And keep adding them to this page whenever and wherever you get them. More than ten is okay, too!*

1.

2.

3.

4.

5.

6.

7.

8.

9.

10.

Say once out loud: *"I am open and willing to receive and try opportunities that increase my wealth and meet my needs."*

**Pick one way to increase your income and take action!**
**Write it on your Page of Promises to Myself at the back of the book.**

# Are You an UNDER-EARNER?
# Take this Quiz & See!

Underearning is "to repeatedly gain less income than you need, or than would be beneficial, usually for no apparent reason and despite your desire to do otherwise." So says Jerold Mundis, author of *Earn What You Deserve.*

Many people want to earn more. They are capable of earning more. But they don't. And – they don't know why.

## Exercise: "Am I An Under-Earner?" Quiz

(Circle the statements that apply to you. Do this quickly without thinking too much about your response. Circle the ones that might apply, even if you are not quite sure.)

1. I often give away my services (volunteering, working more hours than actually paid).

2. It is so hard to ask for a raise (or raise fees) that I just don't do it.

3. I have negative feelings about money and/or wealthy people.

4. I am proud of my ability to make do with little.

5. Someone or something else (IRS, ex-husband) is responsible for my financial situation.

6. I find ways to avoid dealing with money (bartering).

7. I tend to sabotage myself at work (apply for jobs not qualified for or low paying, stop short of reaching goals, change jobs a lot).

8. I work very, very hard (long hours, several jobs). Or, I go into excess and than collapse.

9. I fill my free time with endless chores and tasks.

10. I am in debt with little savings and no idea where my money is going.

11. I have a family history of debt and/or under-earning.

12. I am vague about my earnings (I overestimate or underestimate income; I see gross, not net).

13. I continually put others' needs before my own.

14. I am frequently in financial pain or stress.

15. Recognition and praise are more important to me than money.

Quiz provided courtesy of Barbara Stanny, author of *Secrets of Six-Figure Women: Surprising Strategies to Up Your Earnings and Change Your Life* (Harper Collins, 2002).


## Scoring
If you circled two or more, you're probably earning less than your potential – despite your efforts and/or desire to make more.

If you feel you might be an under-earner, please, please take a look at Barbara Stanny's book, *Secrets of Six-Figure Women*, to find out more about what under-earning is and why it is happening to you. She'll open your eyes and show you how to get out of this exhausting, draining lifestyle and into one of comfort and security.

*(P.S. It's still a good book even if you're not an under-earner.)*

## Exercise: *Today, All My Needs Are Met!*

This is a diary page from a day in your life when the amount you need
$ _____ comes in every month.

Feel how it feels. Then write about it in your diary.

*Dear Diary,*

**Anything you want to add to your Promises Page?**

**BONUS:** Review your **Promises Page** and/or try this…

## Exercise: *Affirmation & Response*

Pick one of these affirmations and write it over and over until you fill up this page.

- The universe always meets my needs. I receive $ _____ a month.
- There is plenty for everyone. I receive $ _____ per month.
- The universe is infinitely abundant. I receive $ _____ per month.
- Make up your own!

After each time you write it, notice if your brain sends a negative thought like "There's not enough for everyone!" Write that down, too. Keep writing the affirmation and your brain's response until the negative thoughts give up. Use an extra sheet of paper if you have to. Say your affirmation aloud.

**Do your Inner Wealth Hypnosis using this affirmation.**

# THIRD ABUNDANCE PARTY!!

(You can move this to any other day this week)

Yea! You made it through the third week!
You looked honestly at your needs
and opened yourself to more income!

Start the party with a quote, blessing or a song.

Choose a person to be the timekeeper.

Give each person six minutes to share
their week of daily Money IN exercises:

1. Say what they loved most.
2. Say what they want to focus on next week.
3. Ask for encouragement and feedback. Let the others help them
   remove any obstacles to staying on the journey.

Then, let the next person have a turn until everybody has a chance to share.

## Activity: *ASK FOR MORE!*

A poet once wrote:

> I bargained with life for a penny
> And life would pay no more
> However I begged at evening
> When I counted my scanty store.
>
> For life is a just employer,
> He gives you what you ask,
> But once you have set the wages,
> Why you must bear the task.
>
> I worked for a menial's wage
> Only to learn dismayed,
> That any wage that I had asked of life,
> Life would have willingly paid.

Wow! You've come a long way already!
Are you feeling more confident about your ability to get your needs met?
Do you see how this works by knowing what you need,
being open and willing to receive that amount,
and then being open to ideas and willing to take opportunities in the world
that are going to help you meet your needs?
It's all right there for you.
Open your eyes! Open your heart!

Well, here's the kicker.
Once you've mastered these techniques,
There's no reason why you can't ask the universe
**for a much larger amount!**
Why stop at your needs being what they are currently?
There's no magic about it.

As you master the concepts in this book,
you can go back and do any of the exercises again.
You can ask for much larger sums of money, knowing that divine abundance
is infinite. And as a child of divine abundance, you can inherit everything by
learning to love prosperity, love yourself, and be connected with divine abundance. **Anything – and everything – is available for you.**

# *No limits!!*

"Some people have trouble with this, fearing they will only feel worse if they
point out to themselves all the things they would like to have and what they
do not have. But that is a spurious fear. Your subconscious already knows
what you want. You have just been hiding it from yourself, that is all, which
only undermines your chances of ever getting it. The fear of not being able to
have it ends up fulfilling itself."
> — Jerrold Mundis in *How to Get Out of Debt, Stay Out of Debt and Live
> Prosperously - Based on the Proven Techniques of Debtors Anonymous*
> (Bantam Books, 1990)

Mundis tells you to look at all areas of your life:

| | |
|---|---|
| **Career** | **Money** |
| **Lifestyle** | **Possessions** |
| **Relationships** | **Creative Self Expression** |
| **Leisure Activities** | **Community** |
| **Personal Growth** | **Education** |

# Exercise: *Your "No Limits" Life*

What are you going to ask for, knowing that everything is available to you? Consider your whole life.

Write notes here:

Take turns sharing with the group something about your "No Limits" life.

## Section II: Money OUT

Living abundantly doesn't mean
spending abundantly on everything.

Living within your means
means your spending will rise
and fall with natural changes in wealth.

Living abundantly means using
what you have
to nurture yourself
in the deepest, most important ways.

# Theme:
# Remembering the Past
# and
# Redesigning the Future

A big BIG problem a lot of people have with money,
especially me,
is a creeping vagueness.
We're not quite sure exactly how much money we make
or we are not sure exactly how much money we spend.

And there are all kinds of good reasons for that!

1. I'm too busy.

2. It's too complicated.

3. My income changes every month .

4. My expenses change too much.

5. I am not detail oriented.

6. I am going through transition-I'll know when it stabilizes. (A personal favorite of mine.  I'm always in transition.)

7. I am not good at it.

8. I am a woman.

9. My dad, my husband, my financial planner or somebody else takes care of all that for me.

We have so many great reasons to stay vague about our money.
But the real reason we do it is
to avoid the feelings that come up
when we really focus and think about money.

What is going on?

The feelings we have can be shame about how much we have
or how little we have
or things that happened when we were children
or shame about wanting money.
We play so many games to avoid really experiencing our feelings about
money .... and about everything else.

When people are addicted to drinking, gambling, shopping, working, sex, or
anything, it's usually a way to create intense feelings-a high-that covers up
all the other feelings we don't want to have.

But **the price of cover-up is our prosperity**, our abundance and our
well-being. "You cannot be a millionaire unless you are willing to feel your
feelings about money," says Phil Laut, author of *Money is My Friend: Eliminate
Your Financial Fears and Take Your First Step to Financial Freedom*. (Ballentine
Wellspring, 1989)


**For the next 21 days we are going to tackle this head-on!**
I have created the **Money & Mood Diary** to cut through the vagueness,
face your yucky feelings associated with money, and move you through it
super fast into a new wave of prosperity feelings.

Each day you write down everything you spend and how you feel about it.
You can also write down things people give you or buy you. Note things you
don't spend and how you feel about that.

Does this bother you at all?
For me, when I think about having to fill out what I spend every day, it makes
me crazy. It triggers all my anxiety issues about money and detailed work -
and I start to hyperventilate.
So, if you're with me ...if you're like that ... I know this is hard.
I know it's really hard. But I really want you to commit to filling out the
**Money & Mood Diary for 21 days**.

It's — trust me on this — it's going to create miracles in your life.
When we bring into the light some of these feelings that are in the dark,
we get **released from dark forces** that are controlling us.
Forces that we don't even realize.
So we're going to bring some of these things into light.
We're finally going to get free.

Ever wonder why a girl who was beaten by her father
ends up marrying a wife-beater?
Ever wonder why the child of an alcoholic marries an alcoholic?
Until you see and release old emotional patterns, they keep pulling you down.
We're finally going to get free of some vicious, old money patterns.

Even if you are doing pretty well with your money
This will make a positive difference.
I make a lot of money running my own business.
I struggled to learn accounting, payroll and budgeting.
But no matter how successful I got, it was as though I was running with
an eight-hundred pound monster on my back.
Bringing this stuff out in the open released the weight
and allowed me to soar to even higher levels of success, wealth and prosperity.

Here are some tips to make the Money & Mood Diary easy:

• **It doesn't have to be perfect.** You know, if you miss something here or there, it's okay. Sure, it would be great if you could write down everything to the penny. That's the goal. But if you don't - if it's not right - Don't quit! Don't give up! Just fall down, get up, and keep going.

• **Just write everything.** One form of self-sabotage I am good at, is making things complicated. I ask, "Do I write in when I charge something on my credit card, or do I write in when I pay the credit card? Because if I write in both, then I've written it in twice." Don't worry about it — just write everything. So write it when you charge it and write it when you pay off the credit card. Always write how you feel each time you're doing anything with money.

• **Your situation isn't different.** Another excuse I would use if I could, would be, "My situation is special." See, I run my own business. I have business expenses and I have personal expenses; I keep them separate. This won't work for me! Yes it will. Just write everything. I put a little "b" or a "p" by the numbers, but it doesn't really matter. It's really very simple. Every time you do something with money during the day, write it down.

- **Remember: Just write everything.** Yep. Automatic payments count, too. ATM fees. Even contributions to your retirement deducted from your paycheck. Taxes. So many ways money leaves our pockets that we don't look at, pretend not to see or feel. Also write down money coming in. When other people pay for your dinner or movie, write it down. When your pay comes in, write it down. Again, if you don't get it perfect, it's okay. Got it?

- **Make it fun.** You're going to love the little conversations you have with yourself in the Mood column. You'll start to hear the little mental background talk that's going on every day in your life around money. This is really going to open up some great stuff for you. And if you're like me, I know I'm asking a lot by asking you to do it. But trust me, it's going to be great. It's going to be a major source of miracles for you!

And guess what? **You're gonna get free from your money monsters!**

# MY MONEY & MOOD DIARY

| $ | What I paid for or received | How I felt before/after |
|---|---|---|
| | | |

## Exercise: *Past Memories*

What do you remember about the way that **money went out** when you were a child?  Did your mother spend and your father save?  Did your father spend and your mother save?  Why did people spend?  Did they spend evenly or in splurges?

Write down the things you remember about the way **money went out** of your household when you were a child.

# MY MONEY & MOOD DIARY

| $ | What I paid for or received | How I felt before/after |
| --- | --- | --- |

## Exercise: *Childhood Story*

Pick a particular memory about the way that money was spent when you were a kid. Describe exactly what happened. Put down how you felt about it. What did you learn?

# MY MONEY & MOOD DIARY

| $ | What I paid for or received | How I felt before/after |
|---|---|---|

# Exercise: *NOW vs. THEN*

Is money going out now like money went out when you were a kid? What is similar in your life now about how money goes out? What do you notice? You may want to look at your Money & Mood Diary to get more ideas.

# MY MONEY & MOOD DIARY

| $ | What I paid for or received | How I felt before/after |
| --- | --- | --- |

## Exercise: *Limiting Beliefs*

Re-read what you wrote on days 1, 2 and 3. What are your limiting beliefs about money going out? What do you accept that you don't want to? Think about your behavior. What must be in your beliefs to make you do that?

## Exercise: *Limit-BUSTING Beliefs*

Pick one of your limiting beliefs about money going out and reverse it. Write out the opposite as if it were completely untrue, completely and totally untrue. For example, if you act as though you must spend to feel good about yourself, write down, "I always feel great about myself – whether or not I spend money." Say it out loud.

**Take your new, unlimited belief about money going out and do your Inner Wealth Hypnosis. Write your notes here:**

# MY MONEY & MOOD DIARY

| $ | What I paid for or received | How I felt before/after |
| --- | --- | --- |

## Exercise: *Future memories*

Read over the new beliefs you wrote down on yesterday's exercise. Close your eyes and imagine a time in the future where this belief applies. What is it like with your new belief? Imagine a specific time and place. What is happening to you? Imagine it in detail. Open your eyes and write down what you saw in your future memory.

Do your Inner Wealth Hypnosis using this future memory inside the right door — your feel-good place. Write your notes here about any ideas or wisdom that come up:

# MY MONEY & MOOD DIARY

| $ | What I paid for or received | How I felt before/after |
|---|---|---|

# Exercise: *Review Page of Promises to Myself*

• Anything that has expired or is done...cross it out!

• Only rewrite promises if you still want to do them and haven't done them yet.

• Look at anything you haven't done and put it on your calendar or To-Do list...figure out when you have time to get it done.

• Things you have successfully completed, cross out in a pretty color or put stars across them.

• Feel the feeling of what it means to you to have accomplished this promise to yourself and what a difference it makes in your life.

• Imagine how your life would be in the future if you hadn't done it. And then imagine how your life is different because you have done it.

• Think of a way to celebrate....Maybe calling a friend and sharing your accomplishment.... Or writing a thank you note to yourself!

# MY MONEY & MOOD DIARY

| $ | What I paid for or received | How I felt before/after |
|---|---|---|

# FOURTH ABUNDANCE PARTY!!

(You can move this to any other day this week.)

Yea! You made it through the 4th week!
You are listening to your daily feelings about spending, facing old feelings about spending, and reprogramming your brain!

Start the party with a quote, blessing or a song.

Choose a person to be the timekeeper.

Give each person six minutes to share
their week of daily **Money OUT** exercises:

1. Say what they loved most.
2. Say what they want to focus on next week.
3. Ask for encouragement and feedback. Let the others help them
   remove any obstacles to staying on the journey.

Then, let the next person have a turn until everybody has a chance to share.

# FOURTH ABUNDANCE PARTY!!

## Activity: Smelling Money!

This wacky exercise comes from Carol Dore, author of *The Emergency Handbook for Getting Money Fast* (Television Publishing, 1999). Get a bag of cash together for the party. Either the hostess can provide it, or everyone can chip in their own cash (Don't worry! You can have it back afterward!)

What you're going to do is put it in a big bowl or a basket and take turns burying your nose in it and inhaling and smelling money. Smelling brings out the most primal feelings in your unconscious - it's like bringing money into your unconscious and becoming one with it.

It's so funny and silly.
Pass it around and have everybody smell the money.

### Tips:
- Feel a sense of gratitude. Remember your connection with divinity as you play.

- It's not about worshipping money—it's about remembering that you are a child of God. Everything is available to you.

- Just the feeling of having cash all over you and smelling it and playing with it stimulates your unconscious sense of abundance and prosperity…and when you walk around with that energy, people offer you jobs, raises, and new opportunities! You feel radiant!

### Other activities:
- Have one person lie down while the others pour the cash over their face and then toss it around… it should feel like it's raining money!

- Sit in a circle and toss the money up in the air so it rains on all of you at once.

# Theme:
# Spending Isn't the Only Way
# to Heal and Feel Better

How I treat my money is how I treat myself.
**Money is all about how we take care of ourselves.**

If it's difficult for you to take care of yourself
like cleaning your house, brushing your teeth,
seeing a doctor regularly,
decorating and caring for your home,
taking care of your clothes and your shoes.

If any of these kinds of things are difficult for you,
it must be very difficult to deal with money
because money is just another way of
taking care of yourself.

Having savings for a rainy day is a way of
giving yourself peace of mind.
If you do not care about yourself and your peace of mind,
You will always be giving away
that savings to somebody else
who asks for it - instead of knowing that it is yours
and it's what you need to care for yourself.
A prudent reserve.

This is a particularly painful issue for me
I have a lot of difficulty in this area.
I was sexually abused by my stepfather
from the age of two to the age of seven.
I was so little, just forming my identity.

The impact on me is that
I learned to be used by somebody else.
I learned that my feelings did not matter.
I learned that I did not matter.

I learned that I was like a crumbled-up tissue
someone used and threw away.
My way of surviving was to become a person
who could say "It doesn't matter. I'm OK."

I could be positive and upbeat no matter what,
no matter how badly I was treated,
no matter how badly I treated myself.

I could still go out and be upbeat and happy
and motivate other people.
But I did not learn how to care for myself
until I healed some of those issues.

# Heal My Money, Heal Myself

And healing was the hardest thing I ever did in my life.
Harder than winning Olympic medals.
Harder than working in the White House.
Harder than having my leg cut off
by far.

I did not start healing until I had my daughter.
When she reached age two,
all the issues I had suppressed
and thought that I did not have to deal with
came up in my face.

I thought I was going crazy some of the time.
But I got help from a counselor at church.
I went to see a hypnotist just to find
some of the memories of what happened
and begin to understand
the bad, damaging, destructive lessons I had swallowed
and undo them.

I worked with a wonderful therapist doing EMDR,
which is a special trauma therapy
for post-traumatic stress disorder
that was used to help many Vietnam Vets.

If you were beaten by a parent in your childhood,
if you were neglected,
if you survived rape or mugging
or anything that traumatizes you,
it's so difficult to care for yourself.

I did not know how I felt most of the time.
Through hard work and healing,
I have learned to care about myself, for myself.

## Are you a shop-aholic?

It looks like you are getting everything you want
but you are not taking care of yourself.

It's like having this monster in your life
stealing all your food out of your fridge
and not leaving you anything to eat.

So you shop and you spend all this money
and then you don't have peace of mind.
You often don't have the things you really need.

A lot of people who end up in financial difficulty
talk about dental work.
Not having the dental work they need
or not having decent underwear,
because they skimp on all of the hidden things
that people cannot see
while they are out buying
expensive clothes and cars and jewelry
like filling their lives up with candy
that does not nourish them.


## What does it take to heal?

I was missing an awareness of what love is.
Think about it.
My torture with sexual abuse started
when I was two years old
and went on for five years until I was seven.

Imagine crying out for help and no one comes.
Day after day after day after day.
Until the part of you that expects help dies.
Until the part of you that can't watch dies.

Until the part of you that can ignore your feelings
Is the only thing left.
The only thing that can grow in that soil.

At the time when kids are forming who they are,
how they think about themselves and
what they know about the world,
I was learning to
be dominated,
to be used,
and that my feelings didn't matter.

I grew up smiling and working hard in a crazy world
but having no idea how to love myself
and having blotted out all my feelings...to survive.

It had always been that way for me—how was I to know
that I was missing something?
How could I love myself?
How could I manage my finances or take care of myself,
when I had no idea of what loving myself or anyone else meant?

When my daughter was two,
memories and flashbacks of what had happened to me
started to come back in strange ways.
I thought I was going crazy sometimes.
It became something I had to deal with,
something I thought I had put behind me.
I tried so many different ways of healing – anything!

Some things worked better than others,
but I kept trying
to find something that would help.
Lots of things did,
but I'm left with this:

My relationship with God is crucial to me
because my original programming as a human being
is so devoid of love, especially for myself,
that when I revert to my habits, instincts, and experience—
it's not good. Not good for me.

**I'm left with this:**
I need to check in with God every day and
open myself up to a love that has nothing to do
with my human experience.
A power that allows me
to transcend everything
that happened to me.

No man, no person, no human being can
make up for what I lost.
It's a gift, really. That I have to turn to God.
I don't have the luxury of
living with ordinary human love—there's none in me.

But when I take time each day
to connect with the presence of God
through meditation, yoga, or playing with my daughter,
when I make that space for myself,
I know that I can live from love.

Instead of fear,
instead of making do,
instead of blocking out my own feelings and
instead of surviving.

I choose to live from love
and I need the presence of God to do that in my life.

**How do you heal?**

# MY MONEY & MOOD DIARY

| $ | What I paid for or received | How I felt before/after |
|---|---|---|

# Exercise: *Your Healing Patchwork Quilt*

It usually takes a whole quilt of healing things—not just one thing.

I have tried:

> Meditation, hypnosis, EMDR therapy, counseling through a church, yoga, building my relationship with God, Feldenkrais, Pilates, twelve step programs, massage, decorating, personal trainer, attending church, chiropractic. (Not to mention workaholism, relationships, drinking, shopping, and other ways to numb the pain – I don't recommend numbness!)

What have you tried for your healing?

What would you like to try?

**Pick one healing thing you want to do and take action! Write it on your Page of Promises to Myself at the back of the book.**

# MY MONEY & MOOD DIARY

| $ | What I paid for or received | How I felt before/after |
|---|---|---|

# Are You an OVER-SPENDER?

Take this Quiz and See!

[Quiz provided courtesy of Olivia Mellan, author of *Overcoming Overspending: a Winning Plan for Spenders and their Partners* (Walker and Company, 1995).]

1. Do you frequently buy things you want, whether or not you can afford them at the moment?

2. Do you have trouble saving money? If you have a little extra available to put in the bank, do you usually think of something you would rather spend it on?

3. Do you frequently buy things to cheer yourself up or to reward yourself?

4. Does more than a third of your income go to pay bills (not including mortgage or rent payment)?

5. Do you frequently juggle bill paying because you always seem to be living on the edge financially? For example, do you tend to pay only the minimum balance on your credit cards?

6. Do you tend to keep buying more of your favorite things – clothes, CDs, books, computer software, electronic gadgets – even if you do not have a specific need for them?

7. If you have to say no to yourself, or put off buying something you really want, do you usually feel intensely deprived, angry or upset?

"If you have four or more YES answers, you definitely have over-spending tendencies," says Olivia Mellan, author of *Overcoming Overspending*. "Heavy bills can result from a temporary emergency, of course. But if you are perpetually deep in debt and have trouble delaying gratification until you can afford what you want, then you are an overspender. Give yourself credit for facing up to this answer – honesty is the first step in recovery."

We'll be working on these issues in a few exercises. For more guidance and support in stopping overspending, you can read her books or visit Olivia on the Web at www.moneyharmony.com .

# MY MONEY & MOOD DIARY

| $ | What I paid for or received | How I felt before/after |
| --- | --- | --- |

# Exercise: *Spending Choices – Gaining Control*

Look at your Money & Mood Diary....

List five situations in which you usually bust your budget and spend more than you can afford:

1.

2.

3.

4.

5.

List five ways to keep yourself out of these situations:

1.

2.

3.

4.

5.

# MY MONEY & MOOD DIARY

| $ | What I paid for or received | How I felt before/after |
|---|---|---|
| | | |

# Exercise: *When You Can't Avoid Situations That Make You Overspend*

The urge to overspend may never go away. But your behavior can change. Just as someone may have the urge to drink, but learns not to, you can learn to watch the feelings rise up, see them for what they are, and choose something else for yourself and your life. There is nothing wrong with the feelings. But when you suppress or try to pretend they are not there, then they gain control – not you.

What do you do? Some things that work--

Breathe…Call a friend who understands…Hum a tune
Say affirmations silently…Count to 50…Hug yourself


List YOUR best five ways to divert the urge to shop when you are stuck in one of these situations:


1.


2.


3.


4.


5.

# MY MONEY & MOOD DIARY

| $ | What I paid for or received | How I felt before/after |
|---|---|---|

# What's Your Spending Type?

[From *Overcoming Overspending: a Winning Plan for Spenders and their Partners*, by Olivia Mellan (Walker and Company, 1995).]

Compulsive spending can be a problem for several kinds of personalities. Do you recognize yourself amongst any of these?

Circle the ones you do, and jot down your examples—

**The money is love spender.** Motive: To show affection to self or others, or to relieve guilt made by an impulse often triggered by stress.

**The blue light spender.** Motive: Bargain hunter. Buys items on sale, almost always without comparison shopping.

**The esteem spender.** Motive: Peer approval. Buys top brand names and prestigious labels from exclusive stores. Wouldn't be caught dead in Wal-Mart.

**The overboard spender.** Motive: Insatiable need, habit or addiction, hobby or collection. Buying is often excessive by normal standards and may be uncontrollable (we're talking QVC addiction or E-bay addiction).

**The "I'll show you" spender.** Motive: Get revenge, show power or feel superior to someone.

**The spin of the wheel spender.** Motive: Thrill of testing one's self against the fate, the stock market or the roulette wheel. Enjoys the intensity of feeling at risk.

## Exercise: *Emotional Money Patterns*

Look over your Money & Mood Diary.
Look at the previous page.
What do you notice about your patterns of behavior
with money and emotions?

What would you like to change about your money and mood patterns?  Do
you have any ideas for changing them?

# MY MONEY & MOOD DIARY

| $ | What I paid for or received | How I felt before/after |
|---|---|---|
| | | |

## Exercise: *Review Page of Promises to Myself*

- Anything that has expired or is done...cross it out!

- Only write promises if you still want to do them
  and haven't done them yet.

- Look at anything you haven't done and put it on your calendar
  or To-Do list...figure out when you have time to get it done.

- Things you have successfully completed,
  cross out in a pretty color or put stars across them.
  Or do something to celebrate that you got it done.

- Feel the feeling of what it means to you to have
  accomplished this promise to yourself
  and what a difference it makes in your life.

- Imagine how your life would be in the future if you hadn't done it.

- And then imagine how your life is different because you have done it.

- Think of a way to celebrate....Maybe calling a friend and sharing your
  accomplishment.... Or writing a thank you note to yourself!

# MY MONEY & MOOD DIARY

| $ | What I paid for or received | How I felt before/after |
|---|---|---|
| | | |

# FIFTH ABUNDANCE PARTY!!

(You can move this to any other day this week.)

Yea! You made it through the 5th week!
You are listening to your daily feelings about spending, learning to control your spending and healing old wounds!

Start the party with a quote, blessing or a song.

Choose a person to be the timekeeper.

Give each person six minutes to share
their week of daily **Money OUT** exercises:

1. Say what they loved most.
2. Say what they want to focus on next week.
3. Ask for encouragement and feedback. Let the others help them remove any obstacles to staying on the journey.

Then, let the next person have a turn until everybody has a chance to share.


**Please report any amazing results to bonnie@bonniestjohn.com
Prizes will be awarded for success stories that inspire.**

# Activity: You Deserve a Medal!

Everybody has had money challenges.
Everybody makes mistakes.
Everybody has worked hard to bounce back.

Think about all the dumb things you've ever done with money and how you bounced back. Pick one money memory and award yourself a medal for falling down and getting up!

Give everyone a turn to say why they deserve a medal.

Everyone should realize there is no shame in having money problems…You can be proud of yourself for dealing with them!

# Theme:
# Spending Reduction
# as Stress Reduction

**Note: You can skip this section
if you are already a great budget keeper.**

OK—are all the accountants gone?
Everybody else, gather round!

I found the simplest budget in the world!

# The Simplest Budget in the World!

Richard Jenkins, Executive Editor of *MSN Money* (formerly Editor in Chief of *Microsoft Money Insider*) came up with a budgeting idea he calls "The 60 percent solution." (You can see his article on the Web at: http://moneycentral.msn.com/articles/smartbuy/basics/8579.asp)

I have tried to enter all my expenses into the computer
and control all the categories.
But once I get them all in, I'm too tired to look at them!
I'm just crazed by the detail work of it all.
God bless you if you can do it.

Everyone says we're supposed to do it.
But I'm not a bookkeeper!
It's great to track our money and our mood diary for 21 days (or 30 days to get a full month cycle) but I can't do it for the rest of my life–
I don't want to do it!!!!   I simply won't do it!!!
Don't make me do it!!!!

#\*$\*%\*!^\*&(@\*\*\*@#$%!!#@^\*#$%@+

(aaahhh – oh, sorry ... Now – as I was saying ...)

**The great news is – you can do the 60 percent solution instead!**

Have you ever said,
> *"I wish someone would just tell me how this is supposed to work!"*
> or
> *"What are 'The Rules' to live by for budgeting?"*

Well, these are the rules!

Richard's 60 percent solution works like this:

Your goal is to get to a position where only 60 percent of your gross income is used for committed expenses that you **have to pay** every month.

That includes your taxes, your mortgage, your cable TV, your clothing, your food, your household expenses, and your insurance premiums. If you tithe, it will have to fit into this 60%, too. In other words, all of your bills, all of your taxes have to fit into 60% of your gross income per month or less.

And you deal with the other 40% of your gross income in 10% chunks:

10% CHUNK #1– Use it on **anything you want** during the month! That's your fun money. Blow it on fun new clothes, meals out, or give it away. When it's gone, you're done for the month. Put it in your checking account with ATM access.

10% CHUNK #2 – Another 10% goes to **short-term savings** for vacations, repairs, insurance, holiday gifts, and other lump sum expenses that come up during the year. These things are not really all that surprising, but we usually don't put them in our budget. They're the "One-time things" that happen a lot. You expect this to be spent during the course of a year. Again, when it's gone, it's gone. Planning carefully helps, but keeping it in a separate account makes it easier to see what you're doing.

10% CHUNK #3 – Another 10% goes to **long-term savings** to be used only for investments that **gain value** and increase your net worth. (Note: a boat or a car is not an investment! These things **lose value** until they are worth almost nothing.) Using it as a down payment on a house, for example, is a good idea.

Once this account starts to grow, you should learn from books on investment and get a good investment advisor. If your investments have some flexibility, you can use your long-term savings for emergency money if you need to. You can get at this money without the tax penalties, unlike the retirement savings chunk that comes next.

10% CHUNK #4 – Finally the last 10% goes into **retirement savings,** preferably taken out before you get your paycheck so you don't see it. Use 401K plans, employer match money and other tax benefits. You can't get at this easily, so it is very, very long term savings.

That's it! That's the whole system.

There are so many things to love about this system:

- **It's simple, simple, simple!** If you keep the money in separate accounts, very little tracking is required. You can see what's in the account and know whether you can go out for an expensive dinner and how much to spend on your vacation. The more planning you do, the better it will work for you. But even when you get sloppy, it will still work.

- **It helps you avoid the biggest mistake most people make:** They think if their income is a little bit more than their monthly bills, they are covered. Then the lump sum expenses usually push them into credit card debt and they struggle to pay it back with high interest. In this trap, saving for your wealth or retirement is only a mirage – you never quite get there.

- **This budget focuses you on the real deal** – you can't afford to pay bills, social security and taxes with more than 60% of your total salary. Shocking, isn't it?

- **This budget isn't focused on dollar values.** Percentages work no matter how much or how little you make. A woman on welfare can start using the same budget principles that will work with a six or seven figure income.

- **Spending percentages means you always live within your means!**

- **For couples, you can pool the money for committed payments,** but keep your fun money accounts separate. If you like, keep your short-term savings and long-term savings separate, too, so that you can make your own decisions about vacation spending and investing, for example. Even if there is only one breadwinner, both of you need to have some of your own money to control.

# Here's how to set up the system:

1. Get two checking accounts. One for the ten percent to spend each month (get an ATM card) and the other is for all the "must pay" bills.

2. Get two savings accounts. One is for short term savings and the other for long term savings.

3. Set up automatic deductions for retirement.

4. Deposit everything into your long term savings account. Only transfer to checking what you have planned to spend. Transfers can be automatic, too. Thus, extra bits of money are saved automatically.

5. Do the worksheet on Day I this week to help you get the amounts right.

# MY MONEY & MOOD DIARY

| $ | What I paid for or received | How I felt before/after |
|---|---|---|

## Exercise: *Are You Ready For The 60% Solution?*

**Enter your monthly gross income:**     $ _____
>  (That is, everything you make before taxes are paid.)

**What do you HAVE TO PAY each month?**
>  (You can get some of these numbers from your Letter To The Universe in Week 3 Day 1. Or – use your paycheck stub plus your Money & Mood Diary to get even better numbers.)

>  How much leaves your check in tax, social security and other deductions?

>                                            $ _____

>  How much do you have to pay for debt?   $ _____
>  How much for housing expenses
>                    (rent, utilities, cable, etc.)? $ _____
>  How much for living expenses?
>  (lunch money, clothes, dry cleaning, groceries, transportation and other usual monthly expenses)        $ _____

**Total Monthly HAVE TO PAY Expenses**
>                    (add it all together):  $ _____

Now use a calculator and divide your total **HAVE TO PAY** expenses by your gross pay (expenses divided by gross pay):      $ _____

>  Move the decimal two places to the right.
>  That's your percentage —
>  (Drumroll please… the moment of truth)
>  **Is it more or less than 60%?**

If it's less – congratulations! You can focus on implementing the rest of the budget system. If not, read on!

# Three Stress Reduction Strategies

If your basic bills are more than 60% of your income, what do you want to do about it?

(This is multiple choice – circle one, two or all three answers)

A. Pay off your debt – and don't borrow more

B. Lower what it costs you to live each month (temporarily)

C.  Increase your income (This is the funnest part!)

**To get peace of mind and prosperity,
you must do one, two or all three of these things
until you can get close to
the 60% solution.**

What are you willing to do?
We'll cover all three Stress Reducers this week.
Read each one and decide what you are willing to do.

# MY MONEY & MOOD DIARY

| $ | What I paid for or received | How I felt before/after |
|---|---|---|

## Stress Reducer A:
# *Pay off your debt–and don't debt anymore*

If you're deeply in debt, you're gonna be using the retirement 10% chunk and the long term savings 10% chunk to pay down your debt as fast as you can. Once your debt is paid off, you can redirect the money back to savings and retirement.

If repayment on debt is taking up more than 20% of your gross income, you really need to get help with it. Paying more than 20% makes it difficult to live and take care of yourself in basic ways. You can negotiate with the people you owe money to. Get help from government approved debt consolidators and/or go to Debtors Anonymous (www.debtorsanonymous.org) for advice and support. You may be surprised at how many options you have – the people you owe money to really do want to help you to repay it. They don't want you to go under.

One of the biggest mistakes people make is waiting too long to ask for help. They struggle. They pay high interest. And they feel ashamed for a long time before finding relief. Some end up in unnecessary bankruptcies. Don't wait–help can provide relief...saving you thousands of dollars. You do not deserve to suffer alone.

## Exercise:  *Debt Repayment*

What I will do to erase my debt:




When I will do it (give yourself a reasonable deadline, look at your schedule):




**Add these things to your Page of Promises to Myself
at the end of the book.**

# MY MONEY & MOOD DIARY

| $ | What I paid for or received | How I felt before/after |
| --- | --- | --- |

## Stress Reducer B:
# *Lower what it costs you to live each month*

If your bills and committed expenses are more than 60 percent of your gross income, then start looking closely at your choices. You may feel everything you do now is absolutely necessary. Yet, living beyond what you can afford, having no savings, no retirement or no money for extras is not pleasant. It is stressful.

**Look around at how you live. Is it worth giving up your peace of mind? The best answer may be to spend less and earn more.** But stubbornly refusing to do either is choosing to deny yourself comfort, abundance and security.

Recently I had a big drop in my income after the tragedy of 9-11. Most of my income at that time came from giving speeches at conferences. Suddenly, not as many people wanted to fly to conferences. The downturn in the economy meant companies had fewer conferences and fewer speakers. Still, I felt lucky to be alive and blessed by so many things money can't buy.

I quickly made some big changes in the way I lived. I left a big house with a gardener and live-in help. I rented it to tenants and moved to a tiny apartment. I don't expect you to feel sorry for me. It's a great apartment in the middle of Manhattan and I am by no means suffering. But most people find it difficult to step down their lifestyle. I jokingly say,
"I have a brand-new dishwasher…but it's in California."
Obviously, I feel the pain of not having things I'm used to having. No matter how much or how little we have, we all hate to give up anything.

**Cutting back hurts – emotionally. Being wealthy requires a discipline to bear that minor hurt for a short period of time, knowing you will have all the external trappings again soon.**

When people don't have a wealth consciousness, they need the trappings – the cars, the clothes, the showcase house – or they feel poor. Sadly, people will refuse to reduce their spending and run up debt very fast while waiting for things to change, looking for a job, or trying to drum up new business. So many stories of how people end up in bankruptcy are people who refused to cut back until it was too late.

If you get in a position where you are losing money every month, going further into debt, cut back as fast as you can. Even if you're taking action to earn more, still cut back and avoid the debt. Remember, it's only temporary. You can always start spending more if you make more.

When your sense of wealth is internal, the ups and downs in the economy don't affect your feeling of being wealthy (at least not as much). Adjusting your spending to match your income is a sign of mastery and long-term financial health – not failure.

In the early days of the 2001-2002 economic downturn, I visited a friend who is an executive at a Fortune 500 company. They were seeing sharp falls in revenue with a worsening trend – and started slashing budgets in quick response.

The training department was at a loose end because no one was allowed to travel there to take classes. No new hires were allowed. I was surprised by the intensity of their reaction when things didn't seem so bad.

However, as the economy worsened, that company's actions looked wise and prudent. It made life uncomfortable for employees, but it meant ensuring the viability of the company over the long haul. When the economy bounced back, they were positioned for success.

**Think of yourself as a Fortune 500 company taking immediate action to balance your books – even while you look for ways to increase your revenue.**

In their book *The Millionaire Next Door*, Thomas Stanley and William Danko reported the results of a study of millionaires in America. They found most millionaires did not drive fancy cars, wear flashy clothes and eat in the fanciest restaurants. The people who did live large were mostly in debt or living off money someone else made. If you're spending more than you earn (or everything you earn) you're not thinking like a millionaire – yet!

**Live simply and invest regularly. That's the true millionaire lifestyle!**

## Exercise: *Lower Your Cost of Living*

Here's a radical thought: *Are there FUN WAYS to cut costs!?!*

• If your housing or car payment is eating you alive, can you trade it in for something less expensive, but more fun? A used convertible, sports car or a tiny condo near the water could be a fun change. Put a lot of stuff in storage and pretend you are on vacation.

• Or if you just have to cut back, pick something fun you can do with a portion of the savings. Stick to it. Bribery works.

• If you have kids or spouse, have a contest to see who has the funnest money saving ideas. Give out prizes for usable ideas—such as one month's savings from any idea that lasts six months. They may think of things like watching TV or playing board games instead of renting videos or going to theatres…and share the windfall!

**What I will do to cut my "have-to-pay" bills:**

**When I will do it** (give yourself a reasonable deadline, look at your schedule):

**Add these things to your Page of Promises to Myself at the end of the book.**

Stress Reducer C
# Increase your income
(This is the funnest part!)

Most people want to make more money — **but they don't want to do anything differently.** They don't want to change jobs, ask for a raise, or change their behavior to get more sales or clients. "Why not?" you may wonder. They think to themselves: it sounds hard, it probably won't work, and I will have to give up things I like about my life now. Not a good idea.

Guess what? The truth is that more income **would** make your life a lot easier and better than it is now. And, the chances are 100% in your favor if you open yourself to abundance and start seizing opportunities. **You are only limited by your beliefs about getting more income.**

For me, moving to a small apartment in New York City was not only a way to cut my expenses — it was a way to take action on increasing my income at the same time. Here I have gotten opportunities to take on consulting contracts, writing jobs, TV work and many fun projects that would not have come my way in San Diego. I was named the Money Coach for the Ricki Lake Show — another opportunity that would not have happened in San Diego. Growing my income meant working harder, learning new skills, and risking failure. Worth it? You bet!

As my income began to bounce back, I enjoyed the feeling of earning more with lower costs of living! I was able to return to better savings habits and enjoy the occasional splurge on clothes or a fancy dinner out. Earning more in combination with lower committed bills for living meant freedom and comfort instead of debt, fear and stress.

## Exercise: *Raise your income*

*Pick at least one of the following activities to get more money in!*

• Do your Inner Wealth Hypnosis. Immediately after opening your eyes, make a list of actions to take. Put at least three actions on your calendar.

• Gather some friends together and ask for their ideas to make more money. Do this at your next Abundance Party if you like...

• Find someone who makes more money than you, doing what you want to do. Ask if you can pick their brain. Take action on what you learn.

**What I will do to receive more money:**

**When I will do it** (give yourself a reasonable deadline, look at your schedule):

**Add these things to your Page of Promises to Myself
at the end of the book.**

# MY MONEY & MOOD DIARY

| $ | What I paid for or received | How I felt before/after |
|---|---|---|
| | | |

# Are you really getting what you want?

When you look at your spending,
the most important question is:
Are you really enjoying what you are getting?

If you're spending a lot of money eating out,
is that really enjoyable to you?
**Is that really what you want?**
Or would you rather economize on eating out a little bit
and get a massage once a week instead?

Once you start really looking
at where your money is going,
you may find that you can
nourish yourself better
by changing your choices.

Maybe you want to have flowers
around your house more often
and if you stop buying Starbucks coffee every morning,
you can easily afford to have flowers around you instead.

**Deprivation won't create abundance.**
**Let me say that again.**
**DEPRIVATION WON'T CREATE ABUNDANCE!**
Putting your money where it fertilizes your soul
Will create abundance for you.
Living within your means
Will create abundance for you.

Use the money you have
To nourish your soul.

# Exercise: *Buying back your soul*

Look at your Mood & Money Diary and see,
Is there something you are paying a lot for
that doesn't nourish you?
Clothes you don't wear, expensive lattes,
or too much of one thing (CDs, books, movies)?

Could you cut back on it and
choose something that really nourishes you instead?

I plan to **stop** spending

$ _____ on _____ .

I plan to **start** spending

$_____ on _____

which truly nourishes my soul!

# MY MONEY & MOOD DIARY

| $ | What I paid for or received | How I felt before/after |
| --- | --- | --- |

# Exercise: *Review Page of Promises to Myself*

- Anything that has expired or is done...cross it out!

- Only rewrite promises if you still want to do them
  and haven't done them yet.

- Look at anything you haven't done and put it on your calendar.
  or To-Do list...figure out when you have time to get it done.

- Things you have successfully completed,
  cross out in a pretty color or put stars across them.

- Or do something to celebrate that you got it done.

- Feel the feeling of what it means to you to have
  accomplished this promise to yourself
  and what a difference it makes in your life.

- Imagine how your life would be in the future if you hadn't done it.

- And then imagine how your life is different because you have done it.

- Think of a way to celebrate....Maybe calling a friend and sharing your
  accomplishment.... Or writing a thank you note to yourself!

# MY MONEY & MOOD DIARY

| $ | What I paid for or received | How I felt before/after |
|---|---|---|

# SIXTH ABUNDANCE PARTY!!

(You can move this to any other day this week.)

Yea! You made it through the 6th week!
You are listening to your daily feelings about spending, facing your spending choices and taking action!

Start the party with a quote, blessing or a song.

Choose a person to be the timekeeper.

Give each person six minutes to share
their week of daily Money OUT exercises:

1. Say what they loved most.
2. Say what they want to focus on next week.
3. Ask for encouragement and feedback.  Let the others help them remove any obstacles to staying on the journey.

Then, let the next person have a turn until everybody has a chance to share.

# SIXTH ABUNDANCE PARTY!!

## Activity: *Get a spending buddy!*

Think of someone you can call when you get the urge to go into debt or overspend or bust your budget. It could be someone in the abundance group, or someone else who is safe for you to let your guard down with. You can agree to do this for each other.

You can share feelings of anger, insecurity, desire for revenge or whatever comes up to make you want to shop or help someone or buy business equipment when you don't have the money for it. If you can't reach your buddy at the critical moment, agree that it is okay to leave a long, rambling voice mail explaining how you feel.

Make sure you discuss this plan with your buddy BEFORE you get into a tough situation. If you can't discuss it now, put it on your Page of Promises to Myself to set up your buddy system (and include your first, second and third choice for buddies).

**You know the urge is coming. Be Prepared!**

## Section III: **Money Supports Me**

Spending less than you earn
can feel like deprivation.

In this section we will look at
how money that sticks around you,
supports you.

Saving gives you the peace of mind,
freedom and future that you deserve.

Let's get inspired about
letting money support us...

# Theme:
# Remembering the Past and Redesigning the Future

I guess when you start out life
disabled, black, female and short,
in a world run by men,
who are usually white, with two legs and tall,
you don't feel ahead in the game.
I always felt like I needed to catch up with everyone else.

I couldn't even keep up with the other kids on the playground.
I was possessed with the desire to know how to get ahead in life
Just to feel like I was even.

I got a job on Wall Street.
I was so happy.
I thought,
"Here I will figure out the secret to getting ahead."

# Bonnie's Story:
# Inner Strength is the Source of Wealth

I worked, slaving over columns headed with "$mm"
which is short for millions of dollars.
Watching them come and go, I realized that
some people earned over a $1 million a year and spent even more.
I thought,
"That's not getting ahead!"

I met people on Wall Street who could
change the bottom line with lease arrangements and tax deals,
but they did not know how to do their own taxes or
how to save money from their own income!

I went to Wall Street thinking I would learn how to get ahead — and realized
nobody would teach you that on Wall Street.
Getting ahead is a commitment to yourself, no matter how much
or how little you make.


I went to Oxford University on a Rhodes Scholarship.
I found out there were so many Rhodes Scholars in Oxford
that they call them "Rhodents."

I thought,
"Economics at Oxford University will really teach me how to get ahead!
I'll learn how the economy works
and invest to be financially free."

But it wasn't so easy.
Despite the fact that I had graduated from
Harvard University, Magna Cum Laude,
I was rejected from the Economics Masters Degree Program!

I decided to simply re-apply until I got in.
No matter how long it took.
I stayed after class one day and asked the professor,
"Do you mind me attending your class even though I'm not officially in the
program? I'm re-applying."
And he said, "I don't mind you attending my class."
He smiled,
"But I remember your application.
Why, I was on the committee that rejected it!
You are not going to get in."

I didn't listen to him—
And I did finish my Masters Degree in Economics
from Oxford University.

I went to Oxford University to study Economics, thinking
I would learn how to get ahead financially.
But what I learned was
The fanciest university in the world
Won't help you learn about money
Unless you have a burning desire inside.
Without inner strength there was no education.

To become financially secure,
you need an inner commitment to it
and a burning desire.
You have to want it enough to fight for it.
The answers are not on Wall Street or at Oxford University;
the answers lie in your heart.

## Exercise: *Past Memories*

What do you remember from your childhood about **money supporting you** or sticking around? What do you remember from your childhood about whether money stayed or whether your family went into debt? Were there ups and downs? Was it always debt? Were there creditors calling? Did your parents save carefully and plan for your college education? Was there a difference between your parents? Did you ever save? Write down everything you remember about money for saving, money for investing, or going into debt.

## Exercise: *Recalling a Lesson*

Think of one particular incident about getting into debt or saving money that is your most powerful memory. Close your eyes, feel it, then open your eyes and describe exactly what happened. Put down how you felt about it. What did you learn then? Would you like to unlearn this lesson?

## Exercise: *NOW vs. THEN*

Does your money stick around now? What is similar now about how you save or get into debt compared to how it was in your childhood? Do you use credit cards like they did?

## Exercise: *Limiting Beliefs*

Re-read the memories you wrote on days 1, 2 and 3. What are your limiting beliefs about **money supporting you**? What do you accept that you don't want to? Think about your behavior. What beliefs must be in your head to make you do that? Write down all your limiting beliefs about **money supporting you.**

# Exercise: *Limit-BUSTING Beliefs*

Pick one of your limiting beliefs about **money supporting you** and reverse it. Make it completely and totally the opposite of the belief that's holding you back. For example, if you feel money always gets taken away when you save it, write down: "My savings and investments always grow and grow, giving me a feeling of security." Say it out loud.

**Take your new, unlimited belief about money coming in and do your Inner Wealth Hypnosis.**

Write your notes here:

## Exercise: *Future Memories*

Read over the new belief you wrote down on yesterday's exercise. Close your eyes and imagine a time in the future when this new belief is true. Absorb the feeling of this new belief. What are you doing differently when money sticks around? How would you like your wealth to grow? Who can you give to? What can you do now that money sticks around and your needs are taken care of? Do you feel less stressed? What things do you enjoy most about it? Settle your mind onto one incident that captures the feeling of your new beliefs. Open your eyes and write it down in detail, as one moment in time.

• Do your Inner Wealth Hypnosis using this future memory inside the right door — in your feel-good place.

• Write action ideas on this page for making money stick around the way you want it to. Don't think. Just write as many ideas as you can.

• Circle one idea – the one that you think is most important and will make the most difference to you. Add it to your Page of Promises to Myself (last page).

## Exercise: *Review Page of Promises to Myself*

• Anything that has expired or is done…cross it out!

• Only rewrite promises if you still want to do them
and haven't done them yet.

• Look at anything you haven't done and put it on your calendar.
or To-Do list…figure out when you have time to get it done.

• Things you have successfully completed,
cross out in a pretty color or put stars across them.

• Or do something to celebrate that you got it done.

• Feel the feeling of what it means to you to have
accomplished this promise to yourself
and what a difference it makes in your life.

• Imagine how your life would be in the future if you hadn't done it.

• And then imagine how your life is different because you have done it.

• Think of a way to celebrate.…Maybe calling a friend and sharing your
accomplishment.… Or writing a thank you note to yourself!

# SEVENTH ABUNDANCE PARTY!!

(You can move this to any other day this week.)

Yea! You made it through the 7th week!
You are facing up to old feelings, getting in touch with your power to bring in money, and reprogramming your brain!

Start the party with a quote, blessing or a song.

Choose a person to be the timekeeper.

Give each person six minutes to share
their week of daily Money Supports Me exercises:

1. Say what they loved most.
2. Say what they want to focus on next week.
3. Ask for encouragement and feedback. Let the others help them remove any obstacles to staying on the journey.

Then, let the next person have a turn until everybody has a chance to share.

**Please report any amazing results to bonnie@bonniestjohn.com
Prizes will be awarded for success stories that inspire.**

## Activity: *Share Your Financial Support Team*

Go around the circle and have each person recommend their financial team (or ask for recommendations).

Name good financial advisors, friendly helpful bank managers, good insurance agents, lawyers for living trust and will, tax preparers, bookkeepers, investment advisors and any other money helpers.

If you don't come up with a number of names to choose from, discuss ideas for getting more names of good helpers who can be trusted.

Each person should choose the helpers for their prosperity team according to their own needs and personality. What works for one person may not work for another.

# Theme:
# Allowing Money to be Part
# of My Support Network

**"St. Peter don't you call me 'cause I can't go;
I owe my soul to the company store."**
— from an old blues song

Debt is slavery.

Recently, on the Ricki Lake Show
every member of the audience wrote down their debt
and put it in a hat.
When they added up all the numbers in the hat,
the figure totaled over $3,000,000!
Now the studio audience of the Ricki Lake Show
is not that big.
I looked around the room and thought about that burden
of debt all of these people were carrying.

I shook my head.

# "I Owe My Soul to the Company Store"

There was one woman with repayments of $1500 per month who
volunteered to work with a debt counselor during the show.
By the end of the show the consolidator had come up with a plan
where she could get her payments
down to about $400 per month. Lower interest, no penalties.
She would be able to repay her debt in about 3 ½ years.
And I thought of her working for 3 ½ years.
Part of the debt was for a car
that had been repossessed and sold at auction.
She still owes $15,000 on a car she'll never see again!
She is going to be working 3 ½ years to pay that off.
And everybody in the audience has a story.
How many years on each sentence?

The old blues song, "I Owe My Soul to the Company Store"
was about people working in a town
with only one factory and one store.
The same people owned both.
So anyone who worked in the factory got credit at the store.
Unfortunately, factory wages didn't match the store prices.
You couldn't buy enough to live on.
So the longer you worked, the deeper into debt you got.

So, the song went,
"St. Peter, don't call me 'cause I can't go,
I owe my soul to the company store."

**How many of us are giving away our souls to the company store,
getting further into debt,
signing away years of our life, without realizing it?**

I wrote this book because I want slavery to be over.
Not just for African-Americans, but for everybody.
For women, for men, for young people.

College kids are now being pushed toward credit cards
and being told: "You should take the credit card now
because once you graduate, you can't get it."
They get credit cards before they have a job, run them up
and enter the workforce tens of thousands of dollars in debt.
Already indentured servants before they even start working.

Getting out of the habit of using debt,
understanding the meaning of debt
is so important to be free.

Of course, not all debt is destructive.
Ask yourself:
Could you sell the item and pay off the debt?
Is the purchase still worth something
After the payments are made?
Debt for things that disappear is a trap.
Debt for a home or a car is okay…
…as long as the payments fit in your budget.

**Living within your means**
**Avoiding empty debt**
**Means owning your self.**

Living within your means
is not being owned by anyone else.

Living within your means
is a gift you give to yourself, of yourself.

Buying everything you want right now on credit is not freedom, It's slavery.

**Peace of mind and freedom**
**Comes from having money stick around and support you.**

# Are You a Compulsive Debtor?
## Take this Quiz and See!

*(Circle the statements that apply to you. Do this quickly without thinking too much about your response.)*

1. Are your debts making your home life unhappy?

2. Does the pressure of your debts distract you from your daily work?

3. Are your debts affecting your reputation?

4. Do your debts cause you to think less of yourself?

5. Have you ever given false information in order to obtain credit?

6. Have you ever made unrealistic promises to your creditors?

7. Does the pressure of your debts make you careless of the welfare of your family?

8. Do you ever fear that your employer, family or friends will learn the extent of your total indebtedness?

9. When faced with a difficult financial situation, does the prospect of borrowing give you an inordinate feeling of relief?

10. Does the pressure of your debts cause you to have difficulty in sleeping?

11. Has the pressure of your debts ever caused you to consider getting drunk?

12. Have you ever borrowed money without giving adequate consideration to the rate of interest you are required to pay?

13. Do you usually expect a negative response when you are subject to a credit investigation?

14. Have you ever developed a strict regimen for paying off your debts, only to break it under pressure?

15. Do you justify your debts by telling yourself that you are superior to the "other" people, and when you get your "break" you'll be out of debt overnight?

"How did you score? If you answered yes to eight or more of these 15 questions, chances are that you have a problem with compulsive debt, or are well on your way to having one. If this is the case, today can be a turning point in your life.

We have all arrived at this crossroad. One road, a soft road, lures you on to further despair, illness, ruin, and in some cases, mental institutions, prison, or suicide. The other road, a more challenging road, leads to self-respect, solvency, healing, and personal fulfillment. We urge you to take the first difficult step onto the more solid road now."

From the web site for Debtors Anonymous (www.debtorsanonymous.org)
> Debtors Anonymous
> General Service Office
> PO Box 920888
> Needham, MA 02492-0009
> 781-453-2743     781-453-2745 (FAX)

In Debtors Anonymous, people come in desperate, terrified,
and unable to sleep at night. What they learn to do
is focus on one day at a time without incurring new debt.

When you encounter a problem
and there's a temptation to go into debt to resolve it,
you ask for help from your friends to talk you out of it,
and to live each day without incurring new debt.
And once you start learning how to do that,
then you can get help to work on your existing debt –
and most importantly,
to make sure you take care of yourself and your needs.

Even if you think your problem is not so BIG, check it out. They have state of the art tools. If they can help people in the worst situations, think what they can do for you!

# Luck can make you rich,
# but it can't KEEP you there.

Have you ever wondered why somebody can win the lottery or get a big inheritance from someone and then blow the whole thing in a few years? They started out poor, got a ton of money and ended up poor. Or someone like Donald Trump can lose all his money in a bad deal where everything goes wrong and then he's rich again in a couple of years.

In my interviews with people who got into bankruptcy or very close, I often noticed a person was doing fine with almost no money and only got into trouble after receiving a five or six figure lump sum. For people who burn through money quickly, getting a large amount is like pouring gas on the flame. It gets so far out of control that the money quickly disappears and the person ends up far in debt before they even know what happened.

## Exercise: *Are You Ready to BE Wealthy?*

J. Paul Getty, one of the richest men in the world,
didn't call his book "how to get rich." He called it *How to Be Rich.*
He explained that if you know how to be rich,
getting rich comes naturally.
If you don't know how to be rich, getting rich won't help.
Are you preparing the space, time and habits
to make wealth feel welcome in your life?

**Do you have any habits that would cause trouble if you got a lot of money? Have you ever gotten a lump sum?**

**What habits of BEING RICH do you have?**

# The Secret of Saving

For so long, I felt like I wasn't a good saver.
I would put money into my savings account for awhile
and then I would need something out of it.
When I took money out of it, I felt like a failure.
I felt like I had failed to save.
After awhile, I didn't want to put money in the account
because I knew I was going to feel like such a failure
every time I took it out.

### The Secret to Saving
### is having more than one savings account!

For example, if you have a savings account for investments and another one for vacations and Christmas gifts, you feel really good taking out the money for the right reason. If you decided to do the 60% Solution Budget, you need two savings accounts: one for short-term savings and one for long-term wealth building. Your retirement accounts are also separate.

Other people recommend more accounts. Phil Laut, author of *Money is My Friend*, says we should have SEVEN savings accounts with seven different purposes:

> 1) Cash flow management; 2) Large purchases; 3) Financial independence; 4) Millionaire investments; 5) Annual income; 6) Taxes; and 7) Generosity.

He suggests the cash flow savings account is where you deposit your checks and any other money you receive. Then you only put into your checking account what is in your plan to spend. This especially helps freelancers, commission sales people and anyone who has fluctuating paychecks. The money stays in your savings unless you specifically pull it out. (Pick up his book if you want the full descriptions of all seven accounts and how to use them.)

If you are starting small and aren't ready to pay bank fees on seven savings accounts, you can try the **Envelope Method**. In addition to your two or three bank accounts, Juliette Fairley recommends saving for specific items in envelopes in your dresser. In her book *Cash in the City* (another fabulous book), Fairley suggests putting leftover money at the end of an evening out into the envelopes – whether it is $2 or $10.

"You'll be surprised how fast you can accumulate $100 in a few weeks from stashing extra dollars in this way," she says. To make it more fun, decorate the envelopes according to what you want: a Fendi purse, a weekend get-away, or treating yourself to a facial. The real payoff is that you'll learn the joy of saving.

So many of us are taught to save without any real end in sight. To get real enjoyment from saving, you need to have clear purposes – some more immediate and others further out. If you are trying to teach saving to your kids, make sure they don't get one savings account with no end in sight. The envelope method is a lot more fun!

**No matter how tight your money is,
stay in the habit of saving!**

## Exercise: *My Savings Accounts*

### Decide how many accounts you need.

The 60% Solution Budget recommends three accounts:
1) Short term
2) Long term
3) Retirement (IRA, 401K, etc)

But you may want more. Do you have trouble when insurance and tax money gets mixed with vacation money? Maybe you want them separate instead of having just one short term account. You can still put 10% of your gross income into short term savings. Just divide it up if that helps you.

Do you want envelope accounts for some little treats? Use money out of your 10% fun money to fill the envelopes. Dream up the accounts you think will work for you...and don't be afraid to change them around later.

### Give them names that stir up positive emotions.

Use names like "Pamper Me Fund," "Bon Voyage," the "Philanthropist" or the "Peace of Mind Account" (Insurance & Taxes).

Set up accounts that inspire you:

1)

2)

3)

4)

**On your Page of Promises to Myself at the end of the book, write yourself a note to start up these savings accounts – and to deposit your paycheck to SAVINGS, not your checking account.**

## Exercise: *Future presents to ME!*

Imagine yourself at the age you would like to retire
(or some age in the future if you are already retired).
Imagine yourself clearly.
What are you doing at that point in the future?
What do you look like?  What do you like to wear?
What do you like to do?

Close your eyes and firmly place yourself in the person
who you will be in the future.

Open your eyes and look around as though you are that person.
**Write about yourself and your life:**

Now, make a list on this page of ten gifts you want –
- Maybe a special purse or designer clothes?
- A certain kind of a car you want to drive?
- Where you want to live?
- Are there classes you would like to take?

Make a list of those presents.  The things YOU (at a future age) want:

1.

2.

3.

4.

5.

6.

7.

8.

9.

10.

Each time you contribute to your retirement fund,
you can cross something off this list!
Your automatic monthly deductions count, too.

It's not just funny money going away into
this boring thing called "retirement."

These are presents to yourself in the future ...........and guess what?

This is the Bargain Discount Sale of all time because
when you put in $100 into your retirement,
you're going to get $200 to spend later!

You can buy presents for yourself at 50% percent off!
*(Actual sale discounts depend on how long you save
and your tax bracket – ask an advisor to explain yours.)*

## Exercise: *My New Relationship with Money*

Pick ONE of the following exercises to do. Do it with your spouse, partner, or children, if you want to.

• Finish the sentence "Money is..."

• Grab a stack of magazines and make a collage depicting your feelings and relationship with money. You can have sections of the collage for: Money In, Money Out and Money Supports Me.

• List all the great things money does to take care of you and what you do to take care of your money in return.

## Exercise: *Review Page of Promises to Myself*

- Anything that has expired or is done...cross it out!

- Only rewrite promises if you still want to do them
  and haven't done them yet.

- Look at anything you haven't done and put it on your calendar.
  or To-Do list...figure out when you have time to get it done.

- Things you have successfully completed,
  cross out in a pretty color or put stars across them.

- Or do something to celebrate that you got it done.

- Feel the feeling of what it means to you to have
  accomplished this promise to yourself
  and what a difference it makes in your life.

- Imagine how your life would be in the future if you hadn't done it.

- And then imagine how your life is different because you have done it.

- Think of a way to celebrate....Maybe calling a friend and sharing your
  accomplishment.... Or writing a thank you note to yourself!

# EIGHTH ABUNDANCE PARTY!!
## It's Your Graduation!!!

Yea! You made it through the whole eight weeks!!
Make this a blow-out good time!!

Start the party with a quote, blessing or a song.

Choose a person to be the timekeeper.

Give each person six minutes to give
their graduation speech.

They might want to include:

1. How I felt about money at the beginning.
2. How I feel about money now.
3. What are some of the best changes in my life.
4. My next key step to wealth and freedom is…
5. My biggest obstacle is…

…and take suggestions.

Then, let the next person have a turn until everybody has a chance.


## Activity: *Design Your Own Graduation Activity—*
## *or just hang loose.*

# Conclusion:  Challenge Countdown

## Days 57 to 60

# Challenge Countdown — Day 57

## Exercise: *Before and After*

**How have you changed by taking the 60 Day Challenge?**

- Stop and look at your Promises to Myself-
- Flip through the exercises in the book-
- Look up the mission you wrote at the start-

**Did you achieve your mission (or better)?**

**What new ways do you take action, feel and think about money that you didn't before the challenge?**

**What are you hoping for NOW, that you weren't hoping for before the challenge?**

## Exercise: *Picture Yourself Five Years from Now*

Now that you've had a chance to gain strength and confidence, and feel good about money and your relationship with money, where do you imagine yourself being five years from now? How is abundance flowing in your life? Close your eyes and imagine a future moment in time that captures your relationship with money five years from now.

**Open your eyes and write a description of that moment you imagined:**

Read your description of that moment ten times out loud. As you read it, if you need to improve it or adjust it to make it feel good, do that. Keep changing it until it feels really, really good.

# Challenge Countdown — Day 59

## Exercise: *Choose Your Next Step*

Congratulations – you're coming into the home stretch!
You've done a fabulous job of building
your money attitude
and strengthening your money muscle.

When you finish the 60 day challenge
you can **celebrate**

---------and take a break---------

before you go on to continue growing your financial education.

But before you close the book and take a break,
I want you to plan some next steps for yourself.

...so many new doors are open for you!
You can learn more about investing,
you can manage your finances in more detail and
you can get some help doing it.

There are a lot of great tools out there.
What I'd like you to do before you close this book,
Is to commit to which plan you're going to get on.

Take a look at your Page of Promises to Myself.
Think about what is important to you.
Then just pick something!
Use the following questions as a guide....

Next, the most important thing for me to tackle is
(Circle one)
- Earning More
- Mastering Spending Choices
- Eliminating Debt
- Learning to Invest and Plan

How I like to learn is –
(Circle as many as you like)
- With another book
- In a class, maybe community college
- On audio tapes
- One-on-one with a counselor
    or financial advisor
- In a 12-step program
- With my friends

Write down the very next thing that you're going to do to improve your financial situation and create abundance in your life after you finish this book. (Turn the things you circled into your next step statement...use the resource list on the next page for ideas.)

I am going to start this next phase of my Money Mastery on the
_____th day of _____.

# Resource List

- If you like to keep learning with your friends, get together and choose from the resources below. Even if each of you choose different next steps, you could still get together once a month for an abundance party!

- For classes about money, you can check with your local community college. Also many local banks and financial advisors offer free seminars. Your employer may host financial seminars – ask your human resources department.

- If you have serious mental health issues or addictions to shopping or debt, you may need a therapist. Get a referral from a trusted friend or doctor.

- Try attending a Debtors Anonymous meeting which covers underearning and overspending as well as debt. It's a bargain…They have great tools and low costs!     (www.debtorsanonymous.org or call 781-453-2743)

- For one-to-one counseling on specific financial issues, you could go to a state-certified, non-profit, debt counseling service. Also, the Financial Recovery Institute (www.financialrecovery.com 877.224.9933) has a program with workbooks and counseling that can take you through the process of improving your financial situation step by step. Karen McCall, founder of the Financial Recovery Institute, also runs teleclasses you can join. Another resource for one-to-one counseling is Olivia Mellan, a fabulous money coach who is especially good with couples. (www.moneyharmony.com or call 202-483-2664 ext. 4)

- For books and tapes, try your local library, bookstore or website. Look at anything written by:

  - Olivia Mellan
  - Gerald Mundis
  - Suze Orman
  - Barbara Stanny

And these particular titles:

Glinda Bridgforth, *Girl, Get Your Money Straight!* (Broadway Books 2002)

Judith Briles, *10 Smart Money Moves for Women* (Contemporary Books 1999)

Cheryl Broussard, *The Black Woman's Guide to Financial Independence* (Penguin 1996)

Juliette Fairley, *Cash in the City* (John Wiley & Sons 2002)

Robert Kiyosaki, *Rich Dad, Poor Dad* (TechPress 1998)

Phil Laut, *Money is My Friend* (Ballantine Wellspring 1989)

Vanessa Summers, *Get in the Game* (Bloomberg Press 2001)

Any ONE of these books would make a positive difference in your life. Don't feel you have to read them all. Pick anything you feel will work for you.

There is no right or wrong next step...so don't let the number of choices overwhelm you. **Pick something that you think you'll like and do it!**

**Thank you** for joining me on this incredible journey.
**Thank you** for allowing me to contribute to your life.

By increasing your wealth and abundance
mine has increased many times over.
By sharing my inner wealth with you
my inner wealth has increased.

I have been challenged to my core to
annihilate old programs,
connect with abundant energy people
and to receive the wealth of the universe.

My income has risen
because **the value I put on myself and my skills went up.**
My habits and awareness have improved
So my money management
**got better and easier at the same time!**
I learned far more than I could fit
Into this little book.

I now pass the baton to you.
In order to reach the next level in your wealth journey,
**find an opportunity to give back to others**
not just with your pocketbook
but **from your inner wealth,**
 your knowledge, your energy and abundance.

I promise you the results in your life will be dramatic.
They say you never learn something fully until you teach it.
I can vouch for that.
So as you look towards your next step
for increasing your wealth,
learning to invest
or implementing some of the new insights you had here,
see how you can **bring some other people along with you.**

Bringing wealth into the lives of others
is a way of giving it to yourself ten fold.
Terri Real, therapist and best-selling author, tells us that
being a child means asking what you can get
and being a grownup means knowing what you have to offer.

**You contain infinite wealth.**
**Go out into the world and share it.**

"As we let our own light shine,
we consciously give others permission to do the same."
— Nelson Mandela

With love,
*Bonnie*

# PAGE of PROMISES to MYSELF

*(Note: If a date arrives and you haven't done it, don't feel bad. It's an opportunity to decide whether or not you really want to do it. If not, cross it off. If you do want to recommit, cross it off and write a new action item with a new date.)*

| ACTION | DUE DATE |
|---|---|
| Find a Venue to Write for Income | 9/30/10 |

162

# PAGE of PROMISES TO MYSELF

| ACTION | DUE DATE |
| --- | --- |